$3.00

Macedono-Bulgarian Orthodox Cathedral
"STS. CYRIL and METHODY"
237 Sackville St.
Toronto 2, Ont.

Faith of Our Fathers

FAITH
OF OUR
FATHERS

The Eastern Orthodox Religion

by

STAN W. CARLSON

with

THE VERY REV. LEONID SOROKA, DEAN UMW

(FOURTH EDITION)

PUBLISHED BY

THE OLYMPIC PRESS

6219 BAKER AVENUE, MINNEAPOLIS, MINNESOTA 55421

OFFICIALLY APPROVED FOR PUBLICATION
METROPOLITAN LEONTY
Archbishop of New York

Primate, Russian Orthodox
Greek Catholic Church of
North America

OFFICIALLY APPROVED FOR PUBLICATION
THE REV. JOSEPH STEPHANKO,
Censor

St. Andrew of Crete Day,
July 17, 1954
New York City, N. Y.

Dated: August 3rd, 1954
Resolution Number 1781
New York, N. Y.
Holy Virgin Protection Cathedral

LIBRARY OF CONGRESS CATALOG CARD NUMBER 55-21996

Printed in the United States of America

THE LUND PRESS, INC.
Minneapolis, Minnesota

Contents

Introduction

The Eastern Orthodox Church, with its history that dates back to the very origin of Christianity, is rich in tradition and the beauty of its ritual. The roots of Orthodoxy are traced to the original teachings of Christ during His days on earth; its ritual adheres to the tenets established by the Twelve Apostles and the early meetings of the hierarchy sitting in councils.

The strength of the Eastern Orthodox Church is shown by its survival through many periods of persecution and its subsequent growth down through the centuries. It is a faith of divine beauty in which the worshippers find tranquility in prayers to God, solace in the ritual and inspiration in the music that is a vital part of the services.

To explore the riches of the Eastern Orthodox Catholic Faith, called the "Mother of Churches," the worshipper should be acquainted with the history, traditions, ceremonies and ritual. Through a searching and complete exposition of the faith, the authors of this book have greatly simplified the understanding of Orthodoxy.

For the layman especially, and for Sunday School use, "Faith of Our Fathers" will prove invaluable. To cultivate a complete knowledge of Orthodoxy, the reader will find all the answers here, simply told, well documented and complete. It is a valuable and much-needed volume that is recommended reading for all members of the Eastern Orthodox Faith.

His Eminence, The Most Reverend LEONTY
Metropolitan of the United States and Canada
Primate of the Russian Orthodox Greek Catholic
Church of North America

I

History

1. EARLY CHRISTIAN BEGINNINGS

The modern Christian Church traces its origin back to the fiftieth day after the Resurrection of Christ — the church day now universally observed as Pentecost. On that historic occasion, the disciples were gathered in Jerusalem; the Virgin Mary and other faithful followers of Jesus were with them.

As recorded in the Book of Acts in the New Testament, the Holy Spirit descended on this assembly, which included about 120 persons, and gave those present the power to speak and teach in the different languages spoken in the world of that time.

Hebrew people from many countries, speaking many varied tongues, had gathered at Jerusalem to observe the Jewish Feast of Pentecost, commemorating the giving of the Ten Commandments of the Law to Moses by God and also celebrating the end of the harvest season. This day was celebrated fifty days after the Passover. Those assembled in Jerusalem were soon marveling at the ability of the disciples and apostles to speak many languages. Three thousand persons became believers and were baptized that day.

As the early church grew and the number of Christians increased rapidly, more spiritual leaders were needed and the Apostles asked the followers of the new faith to select seven worthy men to be ordained as the first Deacons of the church with those selected to be qualified by having wisdom and piety. Stephen, one of the seven selected, was later stoned to death by the Jews to become the first Christian martyr.

Under the leadership of the original twelve disciples, the growing number of Apostles set out to preach the gospel in all parts of the then-known world. The experiences of their missionary journeys, notably those of Paul, comprise most of the books of the New Testament.

The Eastern Orthodox church traces an unbroken line back to the first churches founded by the Apostles themselves, and to the churches that derived their origin from the missionary activities of these first churches. The first Christian centers were the Patriarchates of Constantinople, Alexandria, Antioch, Jerusalem and the Church of Cyprus. The various National Orthodox branches, such as the Russian and Greek Orthodox Churches, were established through missionary work.

The original twelve Apostles included John and James, the sons of Zebedee; Peter, Andrew, Philip, Thomas, Bartholomew (also known as Nathanael), Matthew, Simon Zelotes, James, the son of Alphaeus; Judas Lebbaeus (also called Thaddaeus) and Judas Iscariot, the disciple who betrayed Christ.

Judas Iscariot committed suicide by hanging himself after his betrayal of the Master. Matthias was selected to replace him as the disciples began their mission of preaching the Gospel. Later, the convert Paul became a very important Apostle and he made several long journeys to spread the new faith. Notably, he established the church in Greece.

These early Apostles laid the foundations for the beginning and growth of the Church of Christ. They provided for the ordaining of priests and deacons, preached the word of God, performed the Holy Sacraments and formed an Apostolic council to perfect the Christian doctrine.

At its inception, the church was undivided and it remained united for over a thousand years. Trials and tribulations, persecutions and violent death marked the early growth of the church until the time of Constantine when Christianity prevailed and emerged triumphant.

The controversy over the separation of church and state marked the rise of Christianity from its very beginning. The uncompromising refusal of the early Christians to accord divine honors to the emperors was the cause of prolonged periods of persecution. Even when forced to work underground, however, these churches maintained jurisdiction over themselves.

Constantine, a Roman ruler in the Fourth Century, established Christianity as the state religion and for a period of time that followed, the church maintained its independence. During the fourth century, the emperor became more and more important in religious affairs and the full fruit of this trend came during the sixth century under Justinian who ruled the church and state equally.

During the time of the Byzantine Empire, the Eastern Orthodox Church was in a status of confirmed subserviance to the wishes of the state, a condition called Erastianism, after the theologian Erastus. When the empire began to fall apart, the power of the state in regulating affairs of the church declined.

To properly background the beginnings and growth of the early Christian church, it is pertinent to recount briefly the biographies of the first disciples. Their activities and experiences played a vital part in the development of Christianity.

2. THE APOSTLES OF CHRIST

The first and most illustrious of the Apostles was Peter who preached first in Jerusalem and later in Antioch, the city where Christ's followers were first called Christians. He also preached in many other cities of the Holy Land. It was he who spoke the first sermon after the Pentecost and he was the first of the Apostles to preach the Gospel to the Gentiles. In Rome during the persecutions under the Emperor Nero, Peter was fleeing to safety when he met the Lord carrying the cross near the gates of the city.

Peter asked, "Which way, Oh Lord?" and Christ replied that he was going to Rome to be crucified again. On hearing this, Peter returned to the city, stood trial and was condemned to death by crucifixion. In about the year 65 A.D. he was crucified upside down, requesting this position as he considered himself unworthy of being crucified in the same manner as Christ.

At the first Apostolic Council, held in Jerusalem, the disciple James presided. He became the first Bishop of the church of Jerusalem. James gave to the church the order of Divine Liturgy and the liturgies now used in Eastern Orthodox churches are based on the order of service that he originated.

James was a relative of Jesus and was often referred to as the Brother of the Lord. He was one of the foremost organizers of the early Christian church. James was hated by the Jewish leaders who killed him by throwing him from the roof of a high building and then crushing his head in with blows from a club, at a time when the governor was away from the city. Among the disciples he was known as James, the son of Alphaeus. Later he became known as James the Less or St. James the Just.

Christ and His Disciples

The other James, the son of Zebedee and brother of St. John the Divine, was called a "son of thunder" by Jesus because of his impetuous nature. He once made an ambitious request that he and his brother might sit beside Christ, one on either side, in the kingdom of heaven.

James went to Spain as a missionary and became the patron saint of that country. The shrine of his relics is one of the most celebrated in all Europe. He was put to death by the sword on orders from Herod Agrippa, the son of the ruler who had sought to kill the Infant Jesus. He is now known as St. James the Greater.

Only one of the disciples, Matthew, was a rich man. He had been a publican (tax collector) in Capernaum. After the crucifixion he remained in Jerusalem and wrote the famous Gospel that bears his name. Matthew's gospel is the most important in Christianity and makes the most allusions to the church. He suffered martyrdom in the Near East.

Simon Zelotes was a Canaanite who had been a member of a Jewish party called the Zealots, a group of the First Century who opposed Cyrenius when he attempted to take a census in the year 6 A.D. Simon spread the gospel throughout Egypt and may have carried his missionary work as far as Britain. He suffered death by martyrdom in Persia.

Judas, the brother of James, was probably a cousin to Jesus. He is called St. Jude to distinguish him from the other Judas who betrayed Christ. Judas was also known as Lebbaeus and Thaddaeus. He became a missionary to Edessa and suffered martyrdom in Persia with St. Simon.

Thomas, the doubting disciple, was a carpenter and builder according to tradition. He is called the Apostle to the Indies because of his missionary work in Mesopotamia, Parthia and India and especially Malabar where natives have ancestors converted by Thomas and who call themselves Christians of St. Thomas.

Philip was a Galilaean of Bethsaida. He brought his friend Nathanael to Jesus. Philip was known as an eager seeker after God and he died for his faith at Hierapolis of Phrygia.

Bartholomew, also known as Nathanael, became a missionary in Northern India. He also preached Christianity in Arabia Felix. He met his death by being flayed alive and crucified with his head down, in Armenia.

John, the brother of James and the youngest of the disciples, long outlived all the others. After the crucifixion, John first lived in Jerusalem but later he went to Rome. He was banished to the Greek island of Patmos and while there he wrote the final book of the New Testament, Revelation.

In his old age, John lived at Ephesus in Asia Minor where he founded many churches. Because of his teachings about God, he is known as St. John the Theologian.

Andrew, the first called of the disciples and a brother of Peter, played an important part in the earthly ministry of Jesus. He is known as the Apostle to Southern Russia and the Balkans. Andrew died as a martyr at Patras, Greece by crucifixion on an "X" shaped cross. He hung on this cross for two days before death released his pain and torture. The present-day X-shaped cross is known as St. Andrew's Cross in his honor.

Matthias, chosen to replace Judas Iscariot, spent the first period of his ministry in Judaea. Afterwards, he served as a missionary to Cappadocia and Ethiopia. According to tradition, Matthias was stoned to death in Jerusalem.

The Apostle Paul, while not one of the original disciples, is important in the early development of the church as he became the outstanding missionary of early Christianity. He is known as the Apostle of the Gentiles. Before his conversion, he was named Saul and was a disciple of a learned Pharisee and a bitter enemy of Christianity. Paul wrote fourteen epistles of the New Testament. During his lifetime he made five long missionary journeys. His final voyage was to Rome where he met death in the last of many persecutions. He was beheaded by the sword instead of being crucified because he was a Roman citizen.

3. BLOOD OF THE MARTYRS—PERSECUTIONS

It is symbolic of early Christianity that only one of the disciples of Jesus, John, lived to an old age. The others met violent death in promulgating their faith. During the first three hundred years of its development, the Christian church underwent much hardship and was subjected to many persecutions. In this three-century span there were ten great persecutions.

At the time that Paul was beheaded in Rome and Peter met death by crucifixion in the same city, the first of the great persecutions was being conducted under orders of Emperor Nero. In the year 64 A.D. most of Rome burned and the destruction was blamed on the Christians. Nero ordered the annihilation of all Christians in Rome.

Nero, a demented ruler, had murdered his tutor, his brother and his mother. The fire in Rome had been set to satisfy a whim of obtaining a realistic impression of the burning of Troy by the Greeks. To save himself from the rage of the people, who discovered the origin of the conflagration, he threw the responsibility on the Christians who were already hated by the pagan Romans.

Under Nero's persecutions, some Christians were crucified, some were cut in two by saws, some were sewed up in skins and thrown to the dogs while others were cast to wild beasts as defenseless prey. Some Christians, smeared with tar and pitch, were impaled on stakes and lighted like torches to illuminate Nero's imperial gardens.

In the year 95 A.D., the second persecution took place, ordered by the Emperor Domitian. This ruler considered a belief in Jesus Christ to be incompatible with a belief in the divinity of the Roman ruler so his persecution and purge was directed mainly against high officials of Rome who were suspected of being Christians.

During Domitian's persecutions, the Apostle John was thrown into boiling oil but miraculously he was not harmed by it. He was banished to Patmos. Domitian even sent to Palestine for certain kinsmen of Christ in order to condemn them but when they arrived as poverty-stricken men, he dismissed them as madmen. After this bloody proscription, Domitian himself was stabbed to death by a freedman.

A prolonged period of persecutions took place during the reign of Emperor Trajan. Trajan ordered that no deliberate measures should be taken to hunt out Christians but if they were once summoned before magistrates they were to be forced to choose between sacrificing to pagan gods and death. Prominent among the Christians martyred during this period, which began in the year 106 A.D., was St. Ignatius, the Bishop of Antioch, who was a disciple of St. John the Divine. Ignatius was sent to Rome in chains and was thrown into the Coliseum to be torn to pieces and devoured by wild beasts for the entertainment of the Roman people.

Hadrian, a just emperor, was Trajan's successor. Two learned Christians, the Athenian philosopher Aristides and Quadratus, Bishop of Athens, addressed apologies for their brethren in the faith. As a result of this the Emperor issued orders that Christians should be punished only for crimes and not to satisfy public clamor.

Christian blood was shed in Palestine due to a revolt stirred up by a Jewish rebel, Simon Bar Kochba. Claiming to be a second Messiah, he first successfully defeated Roman armies but the tide of battle turned and he was killed. Many innocent Christians perished because Christianity was still popularly identified with Judaism. Hadrian even obliterated the name of Jerusalem, renaming the town. He raised a temple in honor of Venus on Golgotha and erected a statue of Jupiter on the Holy Sepulchre.

Sixty years elapsed between the third and fourth persecutions. The fourth persecution period began in 166 A.D. Marcus Aurelius, the Roman Emperor at that time, had a strong prejudice against Christians, a prejudice founded mainly on false reports he received concerning their beliefs and way of life. He regarded Christians as natural enemies of the Empire because they gave their first allegiance to God.

Marcus Aurelius resented the calm and courageous attitude of Christians in the face of death as an insult to his own stoic virtue. He subscribed to the viewpoint of the people that Christians were responsible for plagues and other disasters by angering the pagan gods. Persecution of Christians for their Christianity alone became the order of the day under Marcus Aurelius. Among those put to death under his orders was St. Polycarp, the 86-year-old Bishop of Smyrna who was burned alive in the arena at Smyrna.

In 177 A.D. violent persecutions broke out in Southern Gaul. One of the victims at Lyons was Pothinus, Bishop of the town, who succumbed to cruel tortures. Blandina, a slave girl, was gored to death in the bullring. The pagans burned the bodies of martyrs and scattered their ashes on the waters of the Rhone river, calling on the Christian God to cause them to arise from the dead.

The most violent of the ten persecutions was the fifth which took place in the year 202 A.D., during the rule of Septimius Severus. So terrible and violent were the Christian persecutions during this period that many believers thought that the coming of the antichrist was close at hand.

Septimius Severus was at first favorably disposed towards Christians because he had been cured of a chronic disease through the prayers of a Christian slave named Proculus. He had a sudden change of heart in 202 A.D. and issued a decree giving the death penalty to those confessing Christianity.

During this era of persecution, St. Leonidas was beheaded in Egypt and a noblewoman of Carthage named Perpetua was exposed to goring by a mad bull with her baby in her arms. A young girl was thrown into burning pitch but her fortitude was so great that her executioner confessed Christ and followed her to martyrdom.

In 235 A.D. the sixth persecution, directed mainly at the clergy of the church, took place under Maximin. He had succeeded to the throne by murdering Alexander Severus who had been well-disposed towards Christians and had set up a bust of Christ in his chapel beside those of his pagan gods. This persecution was aimed at exterminating the Priests and Bishops in a move to swing the people back to paganism. Severus had maintained friendly relationships with the Christian bishops and Maximim vented his hatred particularly on them.

Called the Bloody Persecution, the seventh persecution was ordered by the Emperior Decius in 249 A.D. Previous persecutions had been localized with the more fanatical enforcing the decrees ruthlessly and the tolerant governors of provinces finding methods of evading them. Under Decius, the persecutions became widespread, severely systematic, and ordered against Christians throughout the entire Roman Empire.

Decius set a time limit for Christians to present themselves to authorities to sacrifice to the pagan gods and receive a certificate of recantation. Many Christians, yielding to torture, were forced to sacrifice against their conscience while others bought certificates to circumvent the pagan worship. Many, however, preferred martyrdom to hypocrisy, including Alexander, the Bishop of Jerusalem; Babylas of Antioch and Fabian of Rome.

The eighth persecution began with a decree issued by Emperor Valerian in 257 A.D. Under this decree, any person found practicing the religion of Christianity was sentenced to death. Valerian also attempted to render Christian communities leaderless by exiling their Bishops. The Bishops, however, not only communicated by letter with their followers but also spread the Gospel to the places of their exile.

Among those martyred during the reign of Valerian were St. Cyprian, the Bishop of Carthage and Sixtus of Rome. The deacon Laurence, according to tradition, was roasted on a red-hot gridiron in Rome after he had pointed to the widows and orphans as the treasures of the church when the governor had demanded the surrender of the Church's treasure.

In 275 A.D. the ninth persecution took place. This was a brutal period but a short one. The tenth and final persecution occurred in 303 A.D. under the Emperor Diocletian, who hoped to weld together the distintegrating empire by restoring uniform religion.

In the earlier persecutions, the target had been the Christians themselves but Diocletian ordered the churches destroyed and had sacred books and Holy Scriptures burned. Bishops and priests were put to death. He published an edict against Christianity in 303 A.D. at Nicaea and followed it with three other edicts in rapid succession. Christians in public office were deposed, the prisons bulged and the blood of martyrs flowed.

Despite all of these persecutions, Christianity grew stronger and continued to spread to all parts of the Roman Empire. Those embracing the faith included many among the nobility. It remained, however, for Constantine the Great to become the first Emperor to become a Christian.

At the beginning of the fourth century, the Roman Empire was divided into an Eastern and a Western division. The top rulers held titles as Augustus and Caesar, respectively.

In the year 311 A.D., Constantine, who held the title as Caesar, was acclaimed as Augustus by his soldiers, following the death of the Emperor who held that title. The right to the title was disputed and Constantine went to war against Maxentius, the military leader who held Italy and who intended to become the ruler of the Western part of the Empire independent of Constantine.

Making war against his adversary in 312 A.D., Constantine came out of his tent on the eve of battle and gazed at the sky. In the heavens he saw a miraculous vision. A cross appeared with a bright light around it and the inscription "By This Sign Conquer."

Constantine interpreted the flaming cross as a vision that his victory depended on faith in the powers of the cross. He immediately ordered that crosses were to be inscribed on all of the army's banners. In the battle of Milvian Bridge which followed, his army was victorious.

Shortly after, in 313 A.D., Constantine, ruler of the West, and Licinius, ruler of the East, held a conference at Milan which resulted in the Edict of Milan which gave tolerance to Christianity throughout the Empire. Under this edict, the freedom of worship for Christians was proclaimed, punishment by crucifixion was abolished and Sundays and other Christian holidays were acknowledged. Just before his death, Constantine became a Christian.

Constantine moved the capital of the Empire eastward to the little city of Byzantium on the Bosphorus. He rebuilt the city and renamed it Constantinople. The city was dedicated in 330 A.D. and no pagan religion was permitted in it. Several churches were built in the city by the Emperor and Constantinople became practically the capital of all Christianity.

Helen, the mother of Constantine, also became a devout Christian. She went on a pilgrimage to Jerusalem when she was eighty years old and there she helped to find the cross upon which Christ was crucified. After it was found she had a great church built on Mt. Calvary in its honor. Pieces of the wood from the cross were sent back to Constantinople. Helen died in 328 A.D. and Constantine died in 337 A.D.

4. THE ECUMENICAL COUNCILS—UNIFIED CHURCH LAWS

Following the recognition of Christianity by Constantine, differences of opinion developed regarding the exact and correct doctrines which Christ had given to the church. Discord over these differences developed.

A firm believer in systematic standardization, Constantine called a meeting of the Bishops and Clergy for the purpose of settling the differences in beliefs and doctrines. Known as the First Ecumenical Council, this meeting was held in Nicaea in 325 A.D. It was attended by three hundred and eighteen men of the clergy including every Eastern Bishop of importance and four Western Bishops. Subsequently, six other Ecumenical councils were convened.

At the First Ecumenical Council, the preeminence of Bishops of the three main centers of the Roman Empire (Rome, Alexandria and Antioch) was approved. As a mark of honor, the Bishop of Jerusalem was added. This council also condemned the heresy of Arius who denied the Divinity of Christ.

This first council proclaimed the true teaching concerning God the Father and God the Son, Jesus Christ. The council formulated canons regulating the church and drew up the first seven articles of the Creed.

At the Second Ecumenical Council, held at Constantinople in 381 A.D., the last five articles of the Creed were composed. The completed creed of twelve articles, which is the symbol of our faith and which is still being used, is called the Nicene Creed.

The second council also rejected the teachings of Macedonius, condemning these teachings as a heresy against the Holy Spirit. Macedonius falsely taught that the Holy Spirit was created by God similarly to angels, being a spirit of a higher degree or order than the angels. The 150 Bishops who attended also granted preeminence to the Bishop of Constantinople.

The reason for the preeminence granted to Rome, Alexandria, Antioch, Jerusalem and Constantinople in the first two councils was due to the fact that the cathedrals of the Bishops in those cities were established by the Apostles themselves. Rome was looked upon as the former capital of the world and Constantinople as the new seat of empire.

The First Ecumenical Council

In 431 A.D. the Third Ecumenical Council was held in Ephesus. This council condemned the heresy of Nestorius who taught that our Lord was only a man with the divinity abiding in Him like in a temple. Nestorius called the Virgin Mary the Mother of Christ and not the Mother of God. Two hundred Holy Fathers attended this council.

The Fourth Ecumenical Council was held 451 A.D. in Chalcedon with 630 Holy Fathers attending. This council's great work was its definition of Jesus Christ as the Second Person in the Trinity as True God and True Man with His divine and human natures distinct without confusion and inseparably united in One Person.

This council condemned the Eutychian party who taught that Jesus was God only and that His divine nature absorbed the human one. This council also decreed that the Patriarch of Constantinople was the single head of the church in Eastern Europe.

In 553 A.D. the Fifth Ecumenical Council convened at Constantinople with 160 church leaders attending. At this meeting the followers of Nestorius were excommunicated and their writings condemned. Nestorius taught that the Virgin Mary's title as Mother of God was erroneous.

The Sixth Ecumenical Council, with 170 Holy Fathers attending, also met in Constantinople, in the year 680 A.D. This council condemned the teachings of the Monothelists who acknowledged only the divine will of Christ while denying the human one. This council adjourned and reconvened in 691 A.D. at the Trula Palace. The council approved the canons of preceding councils.

The Seventh and last Ecumenical Council was convened by Empress Irene and was held at the site of the first council, Nicaea. This council took a stand against iconoclasm and defined the doctrine concerning images and their veneration (not worship) and ordered the images restored in churches. The personnel at this council was composed almost entirely of Byzantine representatives but Papal legates were present. This council met in 787 A.D. with 367 attending. In the seven council meetings, about 2000 representatives of the undivided Christian church participated.

There was growing disagreement between Rome and the other Patriarchates but the separation of Rome did not take place until 1054 A.D. with the final break due to a breach over Filioque dogma.

5. THE GREEK ORTHODOX CHURCH

The Orthodox Church in Greece traces its history back to the time of the Apostle Paul who was the first to preach Christianity in that country. St. Paul preached the Gospel at Philippi, Salonika, Verria, Athens, Corinth and Crete. From these centers, Christianity spread to all parts of Greece.

At the beginning of the Christian era, the Church of Greece comprised a diocese with Corinth as its center. At that time Corinth, known as Achaia, was the most important city in Greece.

After the Roman Empire had been divided by Constantine, Greece and Macedonia constituted the diocese of Eastern Illyricum which was self-governing. For a time, jurisdiction was subordinated to the Roman Bishops but from the time of Emperor Leo the Third, in 733 A.D., Greece was acknowledged as a part of the Ecumenical Patriarchate of Constantinople and thus the history of the Orthodox Church in Greece follows closely the history of the Church in Constantinople.

The Turkish Empire in the Balkans began to fall apart in the nineteenth century as one by one the provinces fought for political independence. Each new state wanted religious as well as national autonomy.

The first of the national Orthodox churches to come into existence was the Church of Greece. The spirit of Hellenism had been kept alive by the

Greek Orthodox Church for several centuries and after the fall of Constantinople to the Turks, the Orthodox clergy of Greece had worked constantly to prepare the people for rebellion against the Turkish yoke. When the Greek nation was ready to wage an unequal war for independence, it was Germanos, the Archbishop of Patras, who raised the standard of revolution and proclaimed the Greek rebellion against the Turks on Annunciation Day, March 25, 1821.

After the successful fight for freedom, it was apparent that the Orthodox Church of the free Greek people could no longer remain under the Patriarch of Constantinople who was still a captive of the Turkish Empire. Thus, from the time of the Greek War of Independence, the Orthodox Church of Greece practically severed all relations with the Ecumenical Patriarchate. Affairs of the church were unsettled until June 15, 1833, when a Synod of Bishops representing the liberated areas of Greece met at Nauplia and declared the church independent.

This action was taken without any previous agreement with the Ecumenical Patriarchate and the result was that the independent Church of Greece was not recognized by the Patriarchate. After many debates and prolonged discussions over a seventeen-year period, the Greek government applied to the Patriarchate for recognition as independent while giving justifications for the previous action.

In 1850, the Ecumenical Patriarchate issued a decree declaring the Church of Greece autocephalous. The Greek Church was to be governed by a Holy Synod composed of five members. In 1852 the parliament of Greece passed acts relating to Bishoprics, Bishops and the Clergy and enacted Statutes pertaining to the Church.

In 1864 the diocese of the Ionian Islands was added to the Church of Greece and in 1881 the dioceses of Thessaly and a part of Epirus were added.

The 1852 statutes passed by the Greek parliament, dealing with the government of the Church, had many faults and were unsatisfactory to the Church hierarchy. The law dealing with the selection of Bishops was particularly unsatisfactory, as under it the Synod could propose three candidates with the government making the final selection from these candidates. The result was that Bishoprics were often filled by those in favor with the government.

Success was not achieved until 1923, under Archbishop Chrysostom, when new acts were passed under which a Synod of Bishops, meeting once a year, replaced the old five-member Synod and constituted the highest authority of the Church. The selection of Bishops was also modified with Bishops selected by the Metropolitans assembled in a Synod.

During the dictatorship of General Pangalos, in 1927, the statutes regarding the Church were again modified with the result that the Greek Orthodox Church was again government controlled with the highest authority of the Church a permanent Holy Synod. Government representatives were to attend all meetings of the Synod.

Some years ago it was unusual to find educated priests among the clergy of Greece but now most of them are seminary educated in one of the twelve theological colleges of the country. There once were around 500 monasteries and convents in Greece and there are still more than 250 of them in the country.

The present Orthodox Church in Greece is governed by a Holy Synod presided over by the Metropolitan Archbishop of Athens. The Patriarch of Constantinople, however, is regarded as the spiritual head of the church and the Holy Chrism used by the Greek Church is consecrated by him. This is a practical arrangement as the Patriarch is still required to be a citizen of Turkey.

6. THE GREEK ORTHODOX CHURCH IN AMERICA

In 1866, the first Greek Orthodox Church in the United States was founded in New Orleans, Louisiana. The Reverend Agapius Honcharenko, a Ukrainian Priest who came to Boston from Athens, Greece in 1865, officiated at the blessing. He was the first Orthodox Priest to settle in the United States and he maintained a chapel in the residence of the Greek Consul-General in New York City.

After the American Civil War, immigration from Greece increased greatly and in 1891 a church was opened in New York. A second Greek Orthodox Church was opened in Chicago, Illinois in 1898.

The number of Greek Orthodox Churches in America increased steadily until in 1910 there were around thirty-five congregations in various parts of the country. Jurisdiction of the Greek Churches in America, under an agreement made in 1908 between the Ecumenical Patriarchate and the Holy Synod of Athens, was given to the Church of Greece but no definite steps were taken to organize an American diocese until 1918 when the Metropolitan of Athens visited the United States.

The Metropolitan of Athens, Meletios Metaxakis, on his visit to the United States, intended to establish an American Archdiocese with Bishops installed in five of the larger Greek centers of the country. His stay in this country was too short to enable him to accomplish this so he designated Bishop Alexander of Rhodostolos to carry out this work.

Bishop Alexander remained in the United States despite important political changes that were taking place in Greece. The affairs of the Greek Church in the United States were greatly complicated by these political changes abroad. On December 8, 1921, Metropolitan Meletios became Patriarch of Constantinople and on May 14, 1922 the decree of 1908 was voided and the Patriarchate of Constantinople took over the jurisdiction of the Greek Churches in America. Alexander was elevated to the rank of Archbishop and in 1923 he consecrated Bishops for Boston and Chicago.

Despite the operations of a conflicting church hierarchy, whose followers sympathized with the Royalist political faction in contrast to the sympathies of the Patriarchal Church for the Venizelists, the Greek Church grew and prospered. Harmony was achieved through the agency of the Metropolitan Damaskinos of Corinth who came to the United States as Patriarchal Exarch in 1930. Archbishop Athenagoras Spyrou of Corfu was appointed to head the Greek Church in America and he arrived in New York early in 1931.

Under the leadership of Archbishop Athenagoras the Greek Church increased to 286 parishes in the United States with others in Canada, Mexico and South America. On November 1st, 1948, Archbishop Athenagoras was elected Patriarch of Constantinople and was succeeded by Archbishop Michael Constantinides of Corinth. He was enthroned in the New York Cathedral of the Holy Trinity on December 18, 1949. With the death of Archbishop Michael in 1958, Archbishop Iakovos was installed as primate of the Greek Orthodox Church in America.

7. THE RUSSIAN ORTHODOX CHURCH

The Apostle Andrew, one of the original twelve disciples of Jesus, preached the gospel of Christianity in Greece and along the northern shores of the Black Sea. He continued his missionary work northward and visited the area known as Skiphia (now Russia). He journeyed as far north as the city of Novgorod.

Russia Accepts Christianity—Baptism at the Dnieper River

Arriving in the region where the city of Kiev is now located, St. Andrew ascended the hills and planted a cross on the mountainside. He then made an historic prophecy that from those hills would shine the light of divine grace, that many churches would be built, that a great city would arise and that Christianity would spread throughout the country.

The cross planted by Andrew was later preserved in a beautiful church built on the mountain in the area that bore his name. St. Andrew continued on through the Caucasus to the southern shores of the Black Sea and then went on to Constantinople. There he ordained priests and deacons and appointed Bishop Stakhy to establish the church hierarchy in Russia.

Andrew was imprisoned in the city of Patara for bringing Christianity to the wife of a local magistrate and her brother. Later he was crucified on an "X"-shaped cross which has since become known as the St. Andrew's Cross. For his work in bringing Christianity to Russia, St. Andrew is known as the Apostle to the Russians.

An interval of nine centuries passed before Christianity received its real start in Russia. In 866 A.D., two princes of Kiev named Askold and Dir became the first Russians to embrace Christianity. The Metropolitan Diocese of Russia dates from as early as the year 891. Many of the Varagians who served in the Imperial body-guard were among the early Russian Christians.

During the reign of Prince Vladimir, who was a zealous heathen, many attempts were made by neighboring nations to convert this powerful ruler to the faiths of their countries. He rejected all overtures until a representative from the Greek Orthodox religion, a philosopher named Constantine, eloquently portrayed the Orthodox beliefs. Vladimir then called his council to discuss this religion as the most suitable one for all Russia.

In 987 A.D., Vladimir sent ambassadors to different countries to examine their religions. These ambassadors ended up in Constantinople where the Patriarch called the clergy together to celebrate a festival according to the ceremonies of the Greek Orthodox faith.

Vladimir's envoys thus attended Divine Services in the Great Cathedral of Haggia Sophia (meaning Holy Wisdom) and returned to Russia with glowing reports. In part they said, "We knew not whether we were in heaven or on earth. For on earth there is no such splendor or such beauty and we are at a loss to describe it. We only know that God dwells there among men and their service is fairer than the ceremonies of other nations. For we cannot forget that beauty." These reports were strengthened by the fact that the Russian ruler's grandmother, Olga, who was renowned for her wisdom, had been baptized in the Greek Orthodox faith.

To serve as an example for his people, Vladimir accepted Christianity and was baptized in the Greek city of Cherson in the Tauride. Returning to Kiev he had his twelve sons baptized and then proceeded to destroy monuments to heathenism. He then issued a proclamation to the people telling them that, rich and poor alike, those who did not appear at the river the next day were to be considered enemies of the ruler.

Multitudes of the people flocked to the River Dnieper the next day, August 1st, 988 and the men, women and children stood in the waters to receive baptism as a nation from the attending Greek bishops and priests. From that date on, the Greek Orthodox faith became the dominant religion of Russia.

In the year 990 A.D., Michael, the Metropolitan of Kiev, went to Novgorod accompanied by several bishops and Vladimir's uncle, Dobrina. They destroyed heathen idols in that city. Many were baptized, churches were erected and priests were ordained. A year later the Metropolitan went into the interior of Russia, journeying as far as Rostov where many were baptized as they accepted Christianity.

As paganism was being overthrown under Vladimir's direction, Christianity spread to all parts of Russia. Vladimir, later canonized by the church, died in the year 1015, thirty-nine years before the final separation of the Western Church from the Eastern Church.

Among the Slavonic peoples, the earliest Christians were two Greek-Slavonic brothers named Cyril and Methodius who were from the Greek city of Solun. The Bulgarians, first of the Slavic nations to accept Christianity, petitioned the Greek Emperor Michael to send Christian missionaries to their country. Cyril and Methodius, the most learned of the Christian Clerics, were sent.

These two brothers compiled the Slavonic alphabet, using the Greek letters as the basis with additional characters added. They then translated the New Testament of the Bible and the books used in the Divine Liturgy into the new language. The Slavonic alphabet, consisting of forty letters, received the name Cyrillic and was used in Russia for the printing of ecclesiastical publications. The Bible, printed in the city of Lvov, capital city of Russian Galicia, by Ivan Fedorov, was the first book printed in Russia.

In the fourteenth century, the headquarters of the Metropolitan was moved from Kiev to Moscow and was given patriarchal dignity by the Patriarch of Constantinople in 1582. Thus, the religious center of Russia replaced Rome as the fifth Patriarchate of Orthodoxy and remained as such in theory even after the office of Patriarch was abolished by Peter the Great in 1721.

Peter the Great set up a Holy Synod to replace the Patriarchate. This synod was composed of Bishops but was controlled by a layman (procurator) appointed by the Czar. Through this action, the Czar became the constitutional ruler of the Russian Orthodox Church.

In 1917 the Holy Synod was replaced by a Patriarch but the vicissitudes of revolution from that time until the present have brought difficult times to the church in Russia.

8. ORTHODOXY IN AMERICA

The Orthodox faith came to America by way of Alaska. Vitus Bering, a Dane who entered the Russian navy in 1704, was chosen by Peter the Great to explore the North Pacific. Before Bering left St. Petersburg in 1725, Catherine the Great, who had succeeded Peter, gave her support to the plan.

After an exploration trip during which he proved that Asia and North America were separate continents, Bering returned overland to St. Petersburg. He then built two ships, naming them the St. Peter and the St. Paul, and sailed eastward from Kamchatka in 1741. During the voyage the ships became separated and were never reunited.

Driven by storms and with his crew dying from scurvy, Vitus Bering landed on an island in the Commander Islands group. This island, where Bering died, was later named for him in his honor.

Bering's voyages clarified the geography of the entire North Pacific and were the basis for Russian claims to the northwest coast of America. Alaska, later purchased from Russia by the United States in 1867 for $7,200,000 was included in Bering's discoveries and became known as Russian-America. The first Russian colonization took place in 1783.

Russian trading expeditions worked down the coast of America and in 1809 a Russian settlement was established in California, located about sixty miles north of San Francisco and named Fort Ross.

The Russians who settled in Alaska and California founded churches soon after their arrival. The first Russian Orthodox missionaries arrived at Kodiak Island, off the Alaskan mainland, in August of 1794. This first mission had a two-fold purpose: to give spiritual service to the men of the Russian Trading Company and to evangelize the native Aleuts. The leader of this first mission was Archimandrit Joasaph.

The Orthodox religion flourished and soon spread to all parts of the Aleutian Islands and to the Alaskan mainland. In Alaska, a Russian Orthodox Church was built on the present site of Sitka in 1815. This edifice became the Cathedral for the first Russian Orthodox diocese on the American continent. Innocentius (Veniaminoff), who was ordained on December 15th, 1848, became the first Bishop of this diocese.

In 1869, two years after Russia had sold Alaska to the United States, a Russian Orthodox Church was built in San Francisco, California and in 1871 Bishop John transferred the seat of his cathedral from Sitka, Alaska to San Francisco.

Bishop Nestor, who succeeded Bishop John, received official permission from the Russian Synod in 1881 to establish his diocese headquarters in San Francisco and property at 1715 Powell Street was purchased for $38,000 for this purpose.

In 1888, Bishop Vladimir came to San Francisco to succeed Bishop Nestor and during his administration the first Russian-Uniat parish, located in Minneapolis, Minnesota, returned to the Orthodox fold. The Very Reverend Alexis Toth was the priest of the Minneapolis congregation which became the Mother Parish of all Orthodox churches in the United States and Canada located east of San Francisco.

Bishop Nicholas succeeded Bishop Vladimir in 1891 and in 1898 Bishop Nicholas was succeeded by Bishop Tikhon who later became the Patriarch of Russia. Tikhon founded the first Russian Orthodox Theological Seminary in Minneapolis, Minnesota in 1905. This seminary building was torn down in 1956 and replaced by a new parish center for St. Mary's Russian Orthodox Church. The first missionary school was also established in Minneapolis in 1897.

Bishop Tikhon also transferred the Episcopal See and its Ecclesiastical Consistory from San Francisco to New York City where the Russian Orthodox headquarters for this hemisphere are still located. Under Tikhon, St. Nicholas Cathedral in New York was built in 1901. He was elevated to the rank of Archbishop in 1903 with jurisdiction over all of North America. Successors to Tikhon were Archbishops Platon and Eudokim. Under Platon's administration more than a hundred new parishes were formed.

In 1919 the Russian Church in America held its first Sobor or general council at Pittsburgh, Pennsylvania. A second Sobor was held in Detroit in 1924 at which time Metropolitan Platon was chosen as the ruling Bishop. He had previously headed the Russian Orthodox Church in America from 1907 to 1914. The same council declared that henceforth the Church in America was to be autonomous.

Metropolitan Platon died in April, 1934. He was succeeded by Bishop Theophile under whose tenure the Federated Russian Orthodox Clubs were founded. After the death of Theophile in 1950, Metropolitan Leonty became head of Russian Orthodox churches of North and South America. He died on May 14, 1965 and was succeeded by Metropolitan Ireney, elected in September, 1965. This jurisdiction has several hundred parishes in the United States and Canada.

THE ALBANIAN ORTHODOX CHURCH

The last of the national Orthodox churches in the Balkan area to come into existence was the Albanian Orthodox Church. Albania declared its independence from Turkey on November 28, 1912, and that status was confirmed at the close of World War I.

A church council convened at Berat in 1922 with a proclamation issued on October 26 declaring the church independent. The Reverend Fan S. Noli, leader of the Albanian Church in America, returned to his homeland to head the Albanian delegation to the League of Nations in 1920 and he subsequently became the Liberal Prime Minister in the new government, assuming that post in 1924.

In 1923, Father Noli was consecrated Archbishop of Durazzo but his plans for the welfare of the church couldn't be carried out due to armed invasion of the country by the Moslem Ahmed Zogu who later became King Zog. Bishop Noli returned to the United States and the Orthodox Church in Albania was finally officially recognized by the Patriarchate of Constantinople on April 12, 1937.

THE ALBANIAN ORTHODOX CHURCH IN AMERICA

The Albanian Orthodox Church in America was organized by Dr. Fan S. Noli in Boston in 1908. Father Noli was ordained in 1908 by Russian Metropolitan Platon and elected Bishop by his people. As has been noted, Bishop Noli returned to Albania to lead his country's fight for freedom. When his work in Albania was interrupted, he spent a period of time organizing Albanian congregations in other European countries.

Bishop Noli returned to the United States in 1930 to resume leadership of the Albanian Orthodox Church in America, serving as Bishop until his death on March 13, 1965. There are thirteen Albanian Orthodox churches in the United States with the Cathedral located in Boston. The Albanian Orthodox Church in America is a completely self governing group with no connection with any church abroad. Another Albanian Orthodox Diocese is headed by Bishop Mark I. Lipa.

THE BULGARIAN ORTHODOX CHURCH

The Bulgarians waged a long drawn out struggle against Imperial Byzantium during the Middle Ages. From 1204 until 1393 the Episcopal See of Trnovo enjoyed independence but conquest by the Turks followed. The Turks, as they did with Orthodox Christians elsewhere, put the Bulgars under the Patriarch of Constantinople and they remained in that status until 1856 when Turkish control relaxed.

On April 3, 1860, Bishop Hilarion gave an open declaration of independence by omitting the name of the Patriarch from the Divine Liturgy. The Bulgars wanted a national church with jurisdiction over their own people everywhere. The Patriarch refused to recognize the new administration and accused the Bulgars of heresy. The Turkish government added fuel to the fire by recognizing a Bulgarian Exarch in Constantinople on March 11, 1870.

Patriarch Anthimios VI excommunicated the Bulgars in 1872 but recognition of this banishment was mainly by the Greeks and not by the Slavic churches. The strained relationship was not remedied until 1945 when communion was restored.

THE BULGARIAN ORTHODOX CHURCH IN AMERICA

The first Bulgarian Orthodox Church in America was built in Madison, Illinois, in 1907. Bulgarian immigration to the United States had increased greatly after 1903 with most of the Bulgarian Orthodox Christians attending Russian Orthodox churches.

In 1922 the Bulgarian Orthodox Mission of the Holy Synod of Bulgaria began attempts to organize the Bulgars. In January, 1938, a Bishopric in the United States was established with Archbishop Andrey, the present head of the churches, appointed in July, 1938.

There are now twenty-three organized parishes of the Bulgarian Orthodox Church in the United States with two more in Canada. There are also fifteen communities that are not yet constituted as parishes. The cathedral is located in New York City and jurisdiction of the Metropolitan includes North and South America and Australia.

THE CARPATHO-RUSSIAN ORTHODOX CHURCH

The people who migrated from the province of Hungary which became the eastern part of Czechoslovakia after World War I make up the American Carpatho-Russian Orthodox Church. Many of those coming to America from Carpatho-Russia after 1886 were Roman Catholics of the Greek Rite whose ancestors had once been of the Eastern Orthodox faith.

A return to Orthodoxy by various Uniat groups began in 1891. It was only in February of 1936, however, that the American Carpatho-Russian Diocese was organized at a meeting of clergy and laymen in Pittsburgh, Pennsylvania.

At a second meeting, held in Pittsburgh in November of 1937, the Most Reverend Orestes P. Chornock was chosen as Bishop and an appeal was subsequently made to the Ecumenical Patriarch, Benjamin I, for canonical recognition.

Bishop Orestes went to Constantinople where he was consecrated Titular Bishop of Agathonicea on September 18, 1938, and given jurisdiction over the Carpatho-Russian Diocese in America. Three Metropolitans, Germanos, Constantine and Dorotheos, were the consecrating Bishops. The following day, the Diocese was canonically established by a decree of the Patriarch.

Bishop Orestes still heads the Carpatho-Russian Church in America with the Diocese including fifty churches and missions. The Cathedral and Seminary are located at Johnstown, Pennsylvania.

THE ROMANIAN ORTHODOX CHURCH

Established as a principate in 1856, Romania became an independent kingdom in 1881. While the country was a principate, an independent church was desired by Prince Couza and laws to establish a national church were passed by the Romanian Parliament in 1864 and 1865. Twenty years passed, however, before recognition was given by the Ecumenical Patriarch.

When Romania became a kingdom in 1881, there was increased incentive for a separate Romanian Orthodox Church and in 1885 Patriarch Joachim IV granted recognition to the national church of Romania.

As a result of World War I, the land area and the population of Romania were greatly increased with the result that the church was strengthened as most of those added were of the Orthodox faith. In 1925 the Orthodox Church of Romania became a Patriarchate.

THE ROMANIAN ORTHODOX CHURCH IN AMERICA

The first Romanian Orthodox Church to be established in the United States was St. Mary's in Cleveland, Ohio, which was organized on August 15, 1904. Earlier, in 1901, two Romanian Orthodox churches had been organized in Canada.

The first Romanian priest to visit the United States was the Reverend George Hertea but his stay in this country was only temporary. Father Moses Balea, who became the pastor of St. Mary's in Cleveland in November, 1905, was the first of the clergy to come to the United States to stay.

Until the time of World War I, all Romanian clergymen came from the Romanian homeland but with the war cutting off immigration, a number of Americans of Romanian origin were ordained by Russian Orthodox bishops in America. Several years after the termination of World War I, the Metropolitan of Sibiu in Transylvania sent eleven priests to America with five of them remaining in the United States permanently.

Beginning in 1911, several attempts were made to organize an American diocese of the Romanian Orthodox Church. On February 24, 1918, a group of delegates who met in Youngstown, Ohio, voted to establish a United States Episcopate. This Episcopate was incorporated and its establishment was confirmed at a subsequent meeting held in Cleveland in April, 1923. The organization, however, did not become active.

The need for a unified Romanian church organization in America became more apparent in 1924 when it was found that three sources of ecclesiastical authority were recognized by Romanian Orthodox clergymen. Those ordained in Romania considered themselves under the jurisdiction of the Metropolitan of Transylvania, those ordained in America recognized the Russian-American Bishop Adam, and those of the clergy in Canada considered themselves under the authority of the Metropolitan of Moldavia.

A Romanian Orthodox Episcopate was organized at a church congress held in Detroit, Michigan, in April, 1929. This new Romanian Orthodox Diocese in America was headed by a provisional commission composed of four priests and eight laymen with the Very Reverend John Trutza of Cleveland as president. Repeated requests were made for a bishop to be sent to the United States.

On March 24, 1935, the Right Reverend Policarp Morusca was consecrated bishop for the American Diocese. He was installed on July 4, 1935, in St. George's Cathedral in Detroit. Under Bishop Policarp the Romanian Orthodox Church in America grew to more than forty parishes.

Bishop Policarp returned to Romania in August, 1939, to attend a meeting of the Holy Synod. The outbreak of World War II shortly after prevented his return to America and the political changes which followed World War II complicated matters further and he remained in Europe. Bishop Policarp is still the canonical head of the American Episcopate.

The American Romanian churches decided recently to return to their original autonomous status. On July 2, 1951, the Right Reverend Valerian D. Trifa was elected as Bishop Coadjutor at a church Congress held in Chicago, Illinois, and the name of the American Diocese was officially changed to the Romanian Orthodox Episcopate (Diocese) of America. The Right Rev. Bishop Victorin heads a Romanian Missionary Episcopate.

The Romanian Orthodox Church in America is divided into five deaneries or districts: Cleveland, Chicago, Detroit, Philadelphia and Canada.

THE SERBIAN ORTHODOX CHURCH

In the year 1346 the first Serbian Orthodox Patriarchate was established at Pec with the consecration of Bishop Ioannikios. This action was protested by the Patriarch of Constantinople and the Serbian Patriarch was not officially recognized until 1375.

The Serbian Patriarchate went into decline after the defeat of the Serbs by the Turks in 1389 and was not reestablished until 1557 when the Turkish Grand Wazir had his brother Makarios, an Orthodox monk, consecrated as Patriarch.

The Ecclesiastical See was suppressed again by the Turks in 1766 and the Slavic Christians went under Greek control where they remained until 1829 when the Serbian revolt against the Turks was successful.

Sultan Murad at first allowed the Serbs to choose the Metropolitan of Belgrade and other bishops but insisted on having the Metropolitan consecrated in Constantinople. Autonomy was granted to the Serbs on November 1st, 1879, by Patriarch Joachim III.

Until the close of World War I, the ecclesiastical and political situation in the area of Europe which is now Yugo-Slavia remained turbulent and complicated. Attempts were made to unite several Orthodox groups into one church with these efforts becoming successful in June 30, 1920, when the union of five autonomous bodies was proclaimed. On November 12, 1920, Metropolitan Dimitriji of Belgrade was appointed Patriarch, uniting in himself the historic titles of Archbishop of Ipek, Metropolitan of Belgrade and Karlovci and Patriarch of Serbs.

THE SERBIAN ORTHODOX CHURCH IN AMERICA

Serbian immigration to the United States reached serious proportions about 1890 and four years later, in 1894, the first Serbian Church in America was founded in Jackson, California, by Archimandrite Sebastian Dabovich. This church was dedicated to St. Sava, the great national Saint of Serbia. Until after World War I, the spiritual welfare of the Serbian Church in America was under the guidance of the Russian Bishop of San Francisco.

In 1900 there were six Serbian congregations in America and in 1906 there were ten. Fifteen years later this number had increased to twenty. In 1926, with thirty-five Serbian churches making up the American Diocese, Archimandrite Mardary Uskokovich was consecrated by Patriarch Dimitriji of Serbia as the first bishop of the Serbian Orthodox Church of America. Under his guidance the diocese increased to forty-six parishes in the United States and Canada. The Cathedral of the Serbian Church, built and opened in 1945, is located in New York.

THE SYRIAN ORTHODOX CHURCH

It is well known that it was at Antioch that the followers of Christ were first called Christians. The Church of Antioch was founded by the Apostle Peter who headed the church there for seven years, from 37 to 44 A.D.

In its early Christian days, Antioch was the richest city of all Syria and the Christians there supported many other communities of new believers.

A Synod held at Antioch in the year 341 issued twenty-five Canons dealing with ecclesiastical matters and these precepts were observed by both the Eastern and Western churches.

St. John of Chrysostom, the most eloquent preacher of all Christendom, was born in Antioch and began his religious career there. During his time, Antioch was a city of 200,000 inhabitants and was called the Athens of the East.

Antioch became the capital of the diocese of Anatolia when the Byzantine

Empire was divided into prefectures by Constantine the Great. Thus all of Syria was included in the jurisdiction of Antioch.

In the seventh century, Syria was overrun by the Arabs but the invaders gave the Christians personal and religious freedom. Damascus was proclaimed as the capital of Syria and of all the Arabian Empire. The Patriarch was required to change his residence from Antioch to Damascus where the Patriarchate is still located.

Due to Moslem domination from the seventh to the eleventh centuries, the Church of Antioch became practically isolated from the other Eastern Orthodox churches. From the end of the eleventh to the beginning of the fourteenth centuries, Syria, along with Palestine, was under the dominance of Crusaders. During this period the Patriarchs of Antioch and Jerusalem lived in exile in Constantinople.

Early in the fourteenth century the Crusaders were expelled from Syria and a Moslem regime was again established. Later, in the seventeenth century, internal troubles in the Church of Antioch caused a division in the population with some becoming Uniate Romans.

For a long period time, the Patriarch of Antioch and his Metropolitans were elected in Constantinople. Now they are taken from the native population and are elected by the Hierarchy of the Patriarchal throne of Antioch. Under the Patriarch there are fourteen dioceses each headed by a bishop.

THE SYRIAN ORTHODOX CHURCH IN AMERICA

In 1878 the first Syrian family of record came to America, but there was little immigration from Syria and Lebanon until around 1890. From 1900 to 1910, about 5,000 persons a year immigrated from these countries to the United States with a peak of about 9,000 arriving in 1913 and in 1914.

The Syrian Mission of the Russian Orthodox Church, founded in 1892, took over the spiritual welfare of the Syrian Orthodox people in the new world, and the first Syrian Church Society was founded in New York in 1895.

Archimandrite Raphael Hawaweeny was brought from the Academy of Kazan in October of 1895 to oversee Syrian church activities in America. In 1904 he was consecrated as Vicar-Bishop to the Russian Archbishop and became the first Orthodox bishop of any nationality to be consecrated in the United States. He served capably until his death in 1915.

In 1914, Metropolitan Germanos, Bishop of Zahle, Lebanon, in the Patriarchate of Antioch, came to America and during his stay in the United States several parishes were organized. In 1924 there were seventeen Syrian Orthodox churches with resident pastors and seven more with a priest in attendance but without parish buildings. The Syrian Mission of the Russian Church consisted of an additional 22 parishes and one mission under the jurisdiction of Bishop Aftimios Ofeish who had been consecrated as Bishop of Brooklyn in 1917 to succeed Bishop Raphael.

For several years, the Syrian churches of America remained under separate ecclesiastical jurisdictions. In 1933, Archbishop Aftimios resigned and

Metropolitan Germanos returned to Beirut where he died in 1934. Bishop Vistor Abo-Assaley, representing the Patriarch of Antioch in the United States, died in September of 1934.

Archimandrite Antony Bashir was appointed as Vicar in America by the Patriarch and he was subsequently elected Bishop of the American Syrian churches. In 1936 he was consecrated in New York by Metropolitan Theodosios of Tyre and Sidon who had been sent to the United States for this purpose.

In June of 1940, Archbishop Antony was elevated to the rank of Metropolitan Archbishop of New York and all North America. He died on Feb. 15, 1966 and was succeeded by The Most Rev. Metropolitan Philip Saliba.

THE UKRAINIAN ORTHODOX CHURCH

In the second half of the ninth century, Slavonic peoples in the vicinity of Kiev laid the foundation for the Kievian state. With the baptism of Prince Vladimir and his acceptance of Christianity, followed by his summoning the citizens of Kiev to a mass baptism, the Christian faith became officially accepted by the Ukrainians in 988.

Later, under Polish rule and subsequent Communist domination, the Orthodox church in the Ukraine became practically non-existent. The church, however, managed to send several bishops to the United States. The Independent Ukrainian Orthodox Church, both in the Ukraine and America, came into being after World War I.

Several hundred thousand Ukrainians had migrated to the United States from 1870 until 1914 and many of the early Ukrainian congregations in this country entered the jurisdiction of the Russian Orthodox Church. A later large migration, between 1945 and 1956, increased the number of Ukrainians in America.

In January of 1919, the Ukrainian National Republic proclaimed the Ukrainian Autocephalous Orthodox Church as the official church of the Ukraine. In October of 1921 a council convened at Kiev with two Archpriests consecrated. One of these, Bishop Lypkiwsky, later became the Metropolitan of Kiev and all the Ukraine. In two years the church had grown to over two thousand parishes and about thirty bishops. The Communist government of Russia, culminating with the deposing of the Metropolitan in 1927, halted the progress of the Orthodox church in the Ukraine.

The Ukrainian Orthodox Church of America held its first convention in 1931. Congregations consisting of former Uniats were added to the Ukrainian Orthodox parishes and the Very Reverend Joseph Zuk was chosen as bishop-elect of the American Diocese in July, 1932. He was consecrated in September of that year and served as the head of the Ukrainian Orthodox Churches in America until his death on February 23, 1934.

Bishop Bohdan Shpilka, who succeeded Bishop Zuk, was consecrated by Archbishop Athenagoras of the Greek Orthodox Church on February 28, 1937. He still serves as the head of American Ukrainian Orthodox Churches under the Ecumenical Patriarch. Technically, Bishop Bohdan is a Suffragan of the Greek Archbishop within the jurisdiction of the Patriarchate of Constantinople. There are forty-five parishes and missions under Bishop Bohdan with the Cathedral located in New York.

The American Ukrainian Orthodox Church was organized about 1919-1920 as an independent church, under the jurisdiction of the Syrian Orthodox Church; it remained in that status until 1924. In February of 1924, Archbishop John Theodorovich arrived in the United States from Kiev, Ukraine. He was chosen bishop-elect of the American Ukrainian Orthodox Church and also head of the Ukrainian Orthodox Church in Canada, Brazil and Argentina. The Ukrainian churches grew in number after the mass migrations to America after World War II.

In a convention held in 1949 at Allentown, Pennsylvania, Archbishop Mstyslaw S. Skrypnik was elected to head the Ukrainian Orthodox Church of America with Bishop Bohdan as Suffragan Bishop. He later resigned from the united church and returned under the jurisdiction of the Greek Orthodox Church.

In October of 1950, the Ukrainian Orthodox Church of America, headed by Archbishop Mstyslaw S. Skrypnik and the American Ukrainian Orthodox Church, headed by Archbishop John Theodorovich, merged to form the Ukrainian Orthodox Church of the United States of America under independent jurisdiction. Bishop Bohdan did not join in this merger and he became head of Ukrainian churches remaining under Ecumenical jurisdiction, now headed by The Most Rev. Bishop Andrei Kuschak.

The United Ukrainian Orthodox Church of the United States has its headquarters in South Bound Brook, New Jersey, and includes 96 parishes in the United States under its jurisdiction. The Most Reverend Metropolitan John Theodorovich heads the church. Metropolitan Dr. Ilarion Ohienko, with headquarters in Winnipeg, heads the Ukrainian Orthodox Church in Canada, which is divided into three dioceses.

OTHER ORTHODOX CHURCHES

There are several other national branches of the Eastern Orthodox Church in the United States. The Russian Synod in Exile, with headquarters in New York, is headed by the Most Reverend Metropolitan Anastassy. This group has more than sixty congregations. The Russian Patriarchal Jurisdiction group, with forty-five churches, is headed by the Most Reverend Archbishop Makary with headquarters in New York.

CHRONOLOGY OF ORTHODOXY
(All dates A.D.)

30 Christ's crucifixion, resurrection and ascension. First Pentecost.
35 Death of Stephen, the first martyr.
36 Conversion of Paul on the road to Damascus. Beheaded in Rome, 67.
42 Beginning of St. Paul's ministry and the writing of his epistles.

46 St. James (the elder) beheaded; first Apostle to die.

52 Apostolic Council of Jerusalem convened.

55 St. Matthew completed his gospel, written in Aramaic.

61 Church established in Antioch; the faithful first called Christians.

62 St. Mark completed his gospel, written in Greek.

63 St. Luke completed his gospel, written in Greek.

64 Burning of Rome. First persecution of Christians by Nero. From 64 A.D. to 305 A.D. there were ten great persecutions. Luke completed the book of Acts and Matthew's gospel was translated into Greek.

96 St. John completed the book of Revelation.

102 Death of St. John after completion of his gospel; last Apostle to die.

325 First Ecumenical Council held at Nicaea.

326 Discovery of the Holy Cross by St. Helena.

381 Second Ecumenical Council held at Constantinople.

431 Third Ecumenical Council held at Ephesus.

451 Fourth Ecumenical Council held at Chalcedon.

553 Fifth Ecumenical Council held at Constantinople.

657 Jerusalem fell to the Arabs. Recaptured by Crusaders in 1099.

680 Sixth Ecumenical Council held at Constantinople.

787 Seventh Ecumenical Council held at Nicaea.

863 Beginning of Christian mission to the Slavic nations.

988 Mass baptism at Kiev; Christianity becomes national religion in Russia.

1054 The Great Separation (schism); establishment of the Western church.

1204 Constantinople falls to the Crusaders. Liberated in 1261.

1346 First Serbian Orthodox Patriarchate established. Suppressed in 1765.

1589 Russian Orthodox Patriarchate established. Suppressed in 1764.

1794 Beginning of Russian Orthodox mission in Alaska.

1809 Fort Ross, California, settled.

1833 Autocephalous Church of Greece established.

1850 Independent Church of Greece recognized by Constantinople.

1866 First Greek Orthodox church in America established at New Orleans.

1885 Romanian Orthodox Church recognized by Patriarch Joachim IV.

1894 First Serbian Orthodox church in America; at Jackson, California.

1895 First Syrian church society in the United States founded in New York.

1904 First Romanian Orthodox church in America; at Cleveland.

1907 First Bulgarian Orthodox church in America built at Madison, Illinois.

1908 Albanian Orthodox Church in America organized in Boston.

1919 American Ukrainian Orthodox Church organized.

1922 Albanian Orthodox Church proclaimed independent.

1924 New calendar (Gregorian) adopted by the Greek Orthodox Church.

1925 Romanian Orthodox Patriarchate founded.

1931 First convention of Ukrainian Orthodox Church in America.

1936 American Carpatho-Russian Orthodox diocese organized.

1955 Eastern Orthodox Church officially recognized as a major faith in the United States by six states. Other states followed with similar recognition.

2

The House of Worship

1. THE ORTHODOX CROSS

The cross is the most prominent of all Christian symbols. It is symbolic of the crucifixion of Christ and His suffering and death for the sins of the world. Constantine, Emperor of the Roman Empire, replaced the symbolic eagles of Caesar with the cross of Christ and this emblem has been the standard symbol of Christian faiths the world over ever since.

The Orthodox cross is distinctive, especially in that it includes the lower bar or foot rest set at a diagonal. There are several historical explanations for this. Beginning in the ninth century, crucifixes began to have the additional footboard in the shape of a horizontal bar in addition to the earlier form which had an upright bar and a single cross bar. This lower bar provided a place for Christ to rest his feet. Byzantine artists used this form of the cross regularly.

The first Byzantine crosses had the added footboard placed horizontally but successive Orthodox crosses put the lower bar at a sharp diagonal. This change took place between the tenth and the eleventh centuries.

One explanation of the symbolism of the Orthodox cross is that it serves as a graphic rebuke to those who held the opinion that Christ did not actually suffer on the cross but only seemed to suffer. The inclined position of the lower bar indicates the intense reality of the suffering in the flesh by Jesus as He hung on the cross. His agony was so intense that His nailed feet wrenched loose the nailed parts of the cross when He thrust one foot down while drawing the other up.

Another religious interpretation is that the right side of the footboard points up to indicate the lightened burden for believers and the left side down to indicate the weighing down of disbelievers. The uplifted right side also indicates that on the second advent of Christ, believers will soar up to Him. Christ's head on the cross is also usually inclined to the right to beckon disbelievers to follow Him, worship Him, and be saved.

Still another interpretation of the slanting footboard is that it symbolizes the part played by the two thieves who were crucified with Christ. The thief on the right repented and is represented by the raised right side of the lower crossbar while the lowered left side represents the other thief who blasphemed Christ during His crucifixion and was condemned.

The extra cross bar at the top of the Orthodox cross represents the inscription board nailed above Christ on the cross. The inscription, "This is Jesus, The King of the Jews," was written in three languages, Greek, Latin and Hebrew.

One explanation sometimes given in Russian Orthodox literature is that the Orthodox cross is a replica of the cross planted by the Apostle Andrew when he looked northward over the mountains of the Caucasus and predicted that a great church would arise. St. Andrew thus became the prophet of the Russian Orthodox Church. The modern St. Andrew's cross, however, is in the form of an "X", the shape of the cross upon which this disciple was crucified.

The Orthodox cross, with its added inscription bar at the top and the added slanting footboard bar below, more fully symbolizes the crucifixion than the commoner simple cross which has only one upright bar and only one crossbar.

2. THE CHURCH BUILDING

Churches are temples of worship—the sanctuaries where divine services are conducted and where prayers are offered to God. In architecture, Eastern Orthodox Churches are usually of Byzantine style, with one or more domed roofs called cupolas. This style of architecture, which developed in the area of Constantinople, reflects the beginnings of the Christian Church in the East and from which the name of Eastern Orthodox is derived.

In the plan of its exterior shape, a church may have any one of several forms. It may be in the form of a cross, shaped like a ship, be star-shaped or circular. Each of these forms has its own symbolic meaning.

A church constructed in the form of a cross denotes that the edifice is dedicated to the Saviour and represents Christ's crucifixion on a cross to redeem sinners. This form reminds us that as Christians we are saved by the Cross of Christ.

A temple of worship built in an oblong shape to resemble a ship denotes that it is through the church that we are saved. Just as the oceans are spanned by ships, the stormy passage of life with its many temptations and tribulations can be safely crossed through the sanctuary of the church and that salvation can be gained at journey's end just as a ship arrives safely in port. The Bishop is likened to the ship's captain who holds the helm, with the rest of the clergy as his sailors. The believers are the passengers. The middle dome on the church alludes to the mast and the cross in the front signifies the flag of Salvation.

A star-shaped church, shaped in eight angles to resemble a star, signifies that through the preaching of the gospel of Christ in the church we are guided along the way to the Heavenly Kingdom, just as the Star of the East guided the first wise men. The church is the star whose light leads to Salvation.

An edifice that is circular in its design signifies that the church, like a circle, is endless. The church is symbolized as abiding to the end of time on earth with a continuation in heaven. The faithful will be forever united with Christ because the church, like the circle, has no beginning and no end.

The cupola domes and the surmounting cross of an Eastern Orthodox Church are reminders that Christ is the head of the church and the lofty curved ramparts are symbolic of heaven above. Each dome is crowned with a cross in emblem of the victory of Christianity.

An Eastern Orthodox Church may have a single cupola or it may have as many as thirteen. When more than one cupola is included in the architecture of the temple of worship, one of the domes is predominant and signifies Christ as the head of the church.

Single Spire   *Five Spires*   *Nine Spires*

When the church has three domes, they represent the Holy Trinity. Five domes represent Christ and the Four Evangelists. Seven domes on the edifice designate the Seven Gifts of the Holy Spirit and nine domes are symbolic of the nine ranks of Angels. When the church has thirteen domes, they denote Christ and the Twelve Disciples.

In all Eastern Orthodox Churches, the altars look to the East, the area of the world where the first Christian Church originated and where the light of Christ first shone forth through the darkness of the world.

3. THE INTERIOR OF THE CHURCH

The interior of an Eastern Orthodox church is composed of three separate parts—the entrance or vestibule, the central nave and the altar or sanctuary.

The entrance area, known as the narthex or vestibule, was used by the catechumens in former times. These included those who were receiving instruction in the Orthodox faith and were preparing for baptism.

The nave area, the middle section of the church, is the church proper where the worshippers gather. In this part of the edifice the pulpit and the choirs are located.

Just in front of the iconostas (the partition that separates the nave area from the sanctuary) is an elevation which has two, three or more steps. The pulpit, sometimes called the amvon, is located in the middle of this area and sometimes projects into a semi-circular form that extends out into the nave. Communion is administered here and the Gospel is read from this elevation. The litany petitions, chanted by the priest or deacon, and sermons are also delivered from this area. Often the choir stalls are placed at both ends of this elevation for use of the singers and readers.

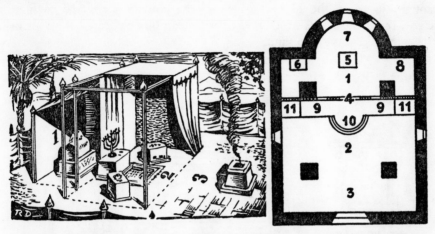

LEFT: *Arrangement of ancient Tabernacle. 1. Sanctuary (Holy of Holies). 2. Altar. 3. Courtyard.* RIGHT: *Arrangement of Orthodox Church. 1. Sanctuary. 2. Middle Area (Nave). 3. Vestibule. 4. Iconostas. 5. Altar Table (Prestol). 6. Oblation Table. 7. Upper Place. 8. Vestment Room. 9. Solea. 10. Amvon. 11. Choir Stalls.*

THE ALTAR

The most important area of an Eastern Orthodox Church is the altar or sanctuary. It is here, strictly speaking, that Divine Services are conducted and the bloodless sacrifice of the Lord's Body and Blood are offered. Only those who have been consecrated by ordination are admitted into the altar.

The central part of the altar contains the Holy Table, also called the Prestol, which represents the Throne of God in Heaven. Only those who are ordained are permitted to touch the altar table which is made sacred by the presence of Almighty God. This Holy Table also represents Golgotha and the tomb of Christ, since His body is placed upon it, The Holy Table is covered by two vestments. The antimins, the cross, the book of the Gospel and the Tabernacle are all kept on this altar table.

THE ANTIMINS

The Antimins, also called Corporals, is a silk or linen cloth with a sketch of the entombment of Christ on it and a relic sewed into it. In addition to representing Christ's lying in the tomb, the Antimins also has images of the four evangelists inscribed on the four corners. The instruments used at the Lord's passion are also portrayed.

In the beginnings of Christianity, the Divine Liturgy was celebrated by the Disciples in private homes or in those synagogues where the Jews accepted the Christian faith. When the first priests were ordained, they celebrated the Liturgy in caves and catacombs as their worship had to be conducted in secret due to the persecutions of heathen emperors. The worship of God was always consecrated upon the graves of martyrs and saints.

To make it possible for a priest to celebrate a Divine Liturgy during a missionary journey, the Holy Fathers of the church permitted each priest to have a replica grave as no Divine Liturgy can be celebrated without being on the symbolic grave of a saint.

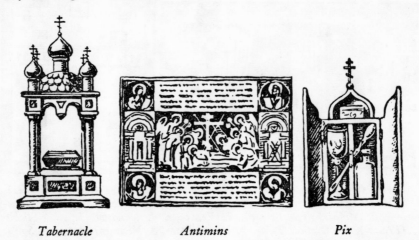

Tabernacle   Antimins   Pix

Thus, to enable a priest to serve without carrying the relics (body) of a saint with him, the Holy Fathers decided to sew a fragment of a relic into a linen cloth or shroud, naming it Antimins, a combined Greek-Latin word meaning in place of a table or grave.

Later, when Christianity was freed from persecutions, the practice of using the Antimins was kept. Some churches, however, still have the relics of a saint kept within the Altar Table. The Antimins is placed on the Holy Table not only in memory of the ancient custom but also in testimony that the Altar has been consecrated by a Bishop and that it is with the blessing of the Bishop that Divine Services are performed on it.

Only a Bishop can consecrate the Antimins and only an ordained deacon, priest or Bishop can touch the table on which it is kept. In consecrating the Antimins, the Bishop anoints it with myrrh (also called Chrism), an oil mixed and blessed by a meeting of Bishops on the Thursday of Holy Week.

Placed on the Altar, the Antimins represents the tomb of Christ and the tombs of holy martyrs upon whose graves the Holy Eucharist was celebrated. The Antimins, an absolute necessity in the celebration of the Divine Liturgy, is kept folded on the Altar Table and is unfolded during the course of the Liturgy. The silk wrapper in which it is kept represents the glory of God's throne.

38

THE CROSS

The cross on the Holy Table signifies that our salvation was achieved through Christ's crucifixion on the cross.

The book of the Gospels, from which the priest reads to the worshippers, points the way to salvation for Orthodox believers.

The Tabernacle, a chest constructed in the shape of a church, contains the blessed sacraments to be used throughout the year when communion is administered to the sick. The vessel in which the holy gifts are carried to the sick is called the Pix.

The Sanctuary also has a small altar placed in the northeastern section, against the wall on the left side of the altar, called the Oblation Table. Here the bread and wine needed for the celebration of Holy Communion are prepared. This preparation, the Proskomide, is the first part of the Divine Liturgy.

The communion elements remain on this small altar until the singing of the Hymn of the Cherubim at which time they are taken by the priest in the Great Entrance through the Royal Doors and placed on the Altar (Prestol).

THE CANDELABRUM

The altar of every Eastern Orthodox Church contains a seven candle candelabrum where candles are kept burning during daytime worship as well as for evening services to symbolize that the Lord illuminates the world with His spiritual light.

Seven is an important number in church symbolism and the use of the seven candle candelabrum indicates the seven sacraments, the seven great Orthodox holidays connected with Christ, the seven Ecumenical councils, the seven gifts of the Holy Spirit, the seven corporal works of mercy, the seven days of the creation of the world and the seven cardinal sins.

In the Eastern Orthodox Church, lighting is increased during the solemn holiday services and decreased when the services are penitential. The symbolic illumination in the church requires oil and wax. Oil, derived from the fruit of the olive tree, indicates that God gives His grace to men and that men in turn must stand ready to offer deeds of love and mercy in sacrifice.

Pure wax, collected from the fragrant blossoms by the bees, when used in candle illumination, indicates that the prayers of mankind, when offered from a pure heart, are accepted by God.

4. THE ICONOSTAS AND THE ROYAL DOORS

The Iconostas is an image screen that has three doors. It forms a high wall covered with sacred pictures that divides the Sanctuary (Altar) from the Nave or main section of the church. Only icons are placed on the Iconostas and these are arranged in a prescribed order.

The middle double doors of the Iconostas are called the Royal Doors; they are so named because the priest comes through them carrying the Communion Cup (Chalice) with Christ Himself the Host. Thus, the Heavenly King passes through the Royal Doors when the procession bearing the elements for the Holy Eucharist passes through.

The Royal Doors are sometimes referred to as the Holy Gates. Only Bishops, Priests or Deacons may enter them and they only at specified times during the liturgy.

The four evangelists, Matthew, Mark, Luke and John, are portrayed on icons on the Royal Doors. They surround the center icon which portrays

Iconostas (Image Screen), showing arrangement of Icons

the Annunciation. An icon portraying the Last Supper, where the Sacrament of Communion was instituted by Christ, is placed above the Royal Doors.

To the right of the Royal Doors is the icon of the Lord Jesus Christ and to the left an icon of Mary, the Mother of God. To the right of the icon of Christ there is usually placed an icon representing the saint or sacred event for which the church is named and to whom the church building is dedicated.

To the left of Mary the icon of some specifically honored saint, usually that of St. Nicholas if the church is not named after this great wonder worker, is placed. Collectively, all of these icons are known as the Deisis tier and each of these prescribed icons are full length single figures. In some Eastern

Orthodox Churches, a series of smaller icons depicting biblical scenes or honoring holy personages is placed below the Deisis tier.

The second icon tier is called the Festival tier and includes icons that illustrate important events in the lives of Jesus and the Virgin Mary. The icon of the Last Supper, directly above the Royal Doors, is included on this tier with the icons on both sides of it portraying the twelve great feast days of the Orthodox church.

The third icon tier includes the twelve disciples with Christ in the middle and John the Baptist and the Virgin Mary on either side of Him.

The fourth tier of the Iconostas is allotted to the Old Testament prophets and in their midst the Mother of God is portrayed holding the Infant Jesus, whose coming to earth was foretold by the prophets.

The fifth tier of the Iconostas, added about the year 1600, is devoted to a crucifix with the Mother of God and St. John the Evangelist on either side as they watched on Golgotha. If there are other tiers, this fifth tier always crowns the others and sometimes reaches to the church ceiling. The arrangement varies when a church does not have five tiers.

In its entirety, the Iconostas presents a great pictorial panorama of the founders and builders of the Christian church, including both the Old and New Testaments. With its deep religious significance, the Iconostas lifts the minds of the worshippers and contributes to a deeper and more sincere spirit of worship.

The entire Iconostas screen is decorated with floral and animal ornaments, symbolic of Paradise with trees, flowers, fruits and birds reaching from earth to heaven to express the union of earthly and heavenly worlds.

The Royal Doors

41

ICONS

Icons (Holy Pictures) serve the same purpose as other embellishments in Eastern Orthodox Churches—they add to the beauty of the Temple of Worship and help make perceptible to the human soul those things which are unseen and eternal.

Icons help the worshipper to concentrate on the high spiritual values and virtues of the holy men depicted. These are symbolically represented and the subjects include God Himself, Christ, the Virgin Mary, Saints and events from their lives.

In the making of an icon, a number of sacred traditions and rules are observed. For some details the colors are prescribed while custom indicates others. Gold and blue are the principal colors used. Icons are always painted on wood with the gilded parts given a base of varnish. The gold leaf for ornamentation is applied with fresh bread and the paint used is dissolved in water with egg-yolk and vinegar added.

In Orthodox tradition, icons are not intended to be realistic paintings of events but rather symbolic interpretations of the great spiritual qualities of the saints such as sacrifice, humility, devotion, faith and love. Icons depicting Saints must clearly indicate what kind of a man (priest, warrior or prince) the person shown was and the deeds leading to Sainthood. Thus, details are often shown very small with servants and attendants appearing as dwarfs and oxen and horses portrayed as calves or small ponies.

In icons, the surroundings are conventional, bodies are abstract and faces are untouched by human joy or sorrow. Prayer, reverence, silence, obedience,

The Vladimir Icon   *The Kazan Icon*

preaching, fear, blame, surprise, lamentation—all are expressed by conventional attitudes and positions of the hands and the heads.

Nature and architecture are used symbolically on icons. A roof with a cupola indicates a church, a single portal represents an entire building, a building symbolizes an entire city and a drapery hanging from one wall to another indicates the interior of a building.

Silhouettes of mountains and trees stress the movement of figures. The sky is often shown on an icon as a triangle with a rainbow at the edge or a scroll with stars and the heavenly bodies which is stretched out or rolled up by two angels. All details of icons have symbolic meanings based on the Scripture, the teachings of the Fathers of the Church, legends, traditions and other theological sources.

For a period of more than 117 years, the Eastern Orthodox Church forbade the having of any representations of Divine or Saintly persons in the church. Icon veneration (but not worship of them) was approved in the year 843. Icons are evidence that the Person venerated lived on the earth and that God, in the person of Christ, became a mortal man to redeem mankind.

PAINTINGS

Murals and frescos contribute to the splendor and beauty of Eastern Orthodox churches. While not indispensable to the decoration of the interior of the church they add greatly to the religious atmosphere.

Frescos (wall paintings) were common during the Byzantine period when much of the Orthodox architecture and art originated. Even small churches of that period had frescos and many of the wall paintings were mosaics, an invention of the Byzantines.

Decorations in the churches during the Byzantine period followed a specified pattern which is still generally followed in present times.

According to this pattern, the arch forming the eastern wall is decorated with the figure of the Mother of God and the Infant Jesus. To the right and left are paintings of the Archangels Michael and Gabriel. On this wall may also be found the figures of St. Basil the Great and St. John Chrysostom, authors of the liturgies. In large churches, several other figures may be included in this section.

The nave (church proper) is highly decorated with frescos and murals. The central dome, which represents heaven, is decorated with paintings of the Lord, who rules the church and the world from His throne in heaven. Angels are shown hovering around the Throne of God, some of them partly enveloped in clouds.

Just below the paintings of the Almighty, Old Testament Prophets are portrayed—the prophets who foretold of Christ's coming to earth. The Four Evangelists, who wrote of the life and teachings of Christ, are shown with their respective symbols.

The inner walls of the nave are also decorated with frescos or full length mosaics. A row on the upper part of the nave walls illustrates scenes from the life of the Mother of God and episodes from the life, miracles, passion and resurrection, appearances after resurrection and the Ascension of Christ.

A second and sometimes a third row of paintings include portrayals of the great saints of the Orthodox Church and scenes from the life of the Patron Saint of the particular church.

Some Orthodox Churches include paintings on the Portico area walls. In earlier times, paintings in this section of the church portrayed the Day of Judgment and similar scenes as a reminder of the Divine Justice to the catechumens.

Stained glass windows did not exist in the time of early Byzantine churches. A modern development, these so-called glowing windows add considerable beauty to the decorations of an Orthodox edifice.

BANNERS

Banners with sacred pictures on them stand at the sides of the front of the church. These serve as ensigns and symbolize the victory of the church over both her inner and outer enemies. These banners are carried at the head of church processionals. They are also symbolic that the entire earthly life is a struggle against the forces that stand in the way of salvation.

Interior of Orthodox Church, shown in cross-section to indicate arrangement of Sanctuary and Altar areas.

5. SACRED VESSELS USED IN THE DIVINE SERVICE

In the Eastern Orthodox service, several special vessels and other sacred objects are an integral part of the service. Included are the Paten, the Chalice, the Asterisk, the Aer, the Spoon and the Spear.

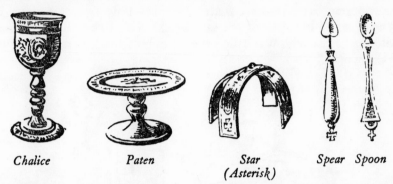

Chalice   *Paten*   *Star*   *Spear Spoon*
                               (Asterisk)

The Paten is a round, flat plate, usually made of silver but sometimes of gold, that holds the bread which is consecrated into the Body of Christ during the liturgy.

The Chalice is a goblet-type vessel of precious metal into which is poured the wine mixed with water that becomes consecrated into the Blood of Christ during the liturgy.

The Star, also called the Asterisk, is placed over the Paten to keep the holy bread and particles disposed around it in a prescribed order and also serves to support the coverings.

Two veils cover the Paten and the Chalice at the beginning and the end of the liturgy. They are symbolic of the swaddling clothes in which the Christ child was wrapped. A third covering, the Aer, is a large veil usually made of the same material as the vestments of the priest which covers the Chalice and the Paten during the Divine Liturgy. The Aer symbolizes the linen cloth (shroud) in which the Body of Christ was wrapped for burial by Joseph of Arimathea. It also symbolizes the Heavens which God created and His Glory and Grace which cover the entire world.

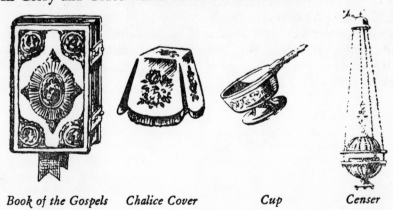

Book of the Gospels   Chalice Cover   Cup   Censer

45

The Spoon is used to convey the Holy Gifts (the Body and Blood of Christ) into the mouths of the worshippers in Holy Communion.

The Spear is employed in taking the Agnets and other portions from the loaves of altar bread and for breaking the bread. The Agnets is the cube lifted out of the altar bread (called prosphora) and designated for the mystical transubstantiation into the Body of Christ. This Agnets is often referred to as the "Lamb" in token of the sacrificial lamb of the Old Testament and symbolic of Christ who was called the "Lamb of God, that taketh away the sin of the world."

Oblation Table, showing paten cover, star, paten, chalice, cup and Aer (Veil).   *Altar (Prestol), showing Book of the Gospels, Antimins, Tabernacle, Pix and Cross.*

The Oblation Table is placed against the wall on the left side of the sanctuary. It is here that the elements to be used in the Divine Liturgy (the Holy Eucharist) are prepared before the beginning of the service. During the procession of the Great Entrance, these Holy Gifts are brought from the Oblation Table to the Altar (Prestol).

The altar proper (Prestol) is located in the center of the sanctuary. The elements for the sacrifice of the Eucharist (the bread and wine) are transubstantiated here into the true body and blood of Christ at the time of consecration during the Divine Liturgy.

46

6. SACRED VESTMENTS

There are many vestments and accessories worn by deacons, priests and bishops of the Eastern Orthodox Church. Members of the clergy are vested in sacred garments appropriate to their respective ranks.

These vestments include the alb or dalmatic, the stole, cuffs, zone, chasuble, the pall and the miter.

Dalmatic   *Bishop's Dalmatic*   *Chasuble*
(Sakkos)   *(Phelone)*

Deacons wear an alb or dalmatic, a long straight vestment reaching to the feet. It covers the entire person and has wide sleeves. An alb is always made of material that is light in color and symbolizes purity—the pure and spotless life and the spiritual joy which flows from the wearer. The alb is worn under the chasuble, a large garment without sleeves which is short in front with an opening for the head. The chasuble is the chief vestment of the priest.

The stole worn by a deacon is a long band of material worn over the left shoulder and sometimes crossed upon the breast and back. A sub-deacon wears the stole always crossed for convenience in carrying out his duties. A deacon binds the stole about himself in the form of a cross shortly before the holy gifts are consecrated.

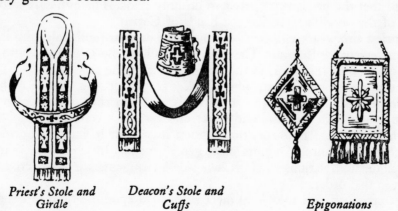

Priest's Stole and   *Deacon's Stole and*
Girdle   *Cuffs*   *Epigonations*

Crossing the stole symbolizes the wings of angels who serve about the altar. The deacons themselves represent two orders of angels, Cherubim and Seraphim. Stoles are sometimes embroidered with angelic songs. During the reading of the litanies in the divine service, the deacon holds the stole in his right hand to symbolize a prayer being offered to heaven.

Deacons also wear cuffs for convenience during the service. These cuffs serve to remind him that he must not put his trust in his own strength alone but in the strength and right hand of the Lord.

The dalmatic worn by priests is similar to that worn by deacons with the exception that it has narrow sleeves and the material is of lighter weight. The stole worn by priests is a long double stole which passes around the neck. This stole symbolizes the consecrated grace of the priesthood and indicates that a priest has double grace as compared to a deacon.

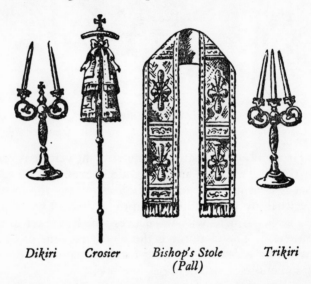

Dikiri   *Crosier*   *Bishop's Stole*   *Trikiri*
                         (Pall)

The stole must be worn by a priest in the performance of any service. Priests also wear the cuffs to symbolize that the priest's hands are tied against sin and that the priest is prepared to do only good. The cuffs are also symbolic of the bonds which tied the hands of Christ.

A priest also wears a girdle tied around the dalmatic and stole—this is worn for convenience in serving. The girdle symbolizes the gift of strength given by God to assist the priest in the performance of the service.

The vestment of a priest, which differs from that of a deacon or bishop, is called a chasuble. This garment, which is without sleeves and short in front, has an opening for the head and is put on over other vestments.

Other vestment ornaments that a priest may wear to indicate outstanding service to the church (honors bestowed on priests by the bishop) include the epigonation, various headpieces, a side adornment, a jeweled cross and a miter, in that order.

The epigonation is an oblong piece suspended upon the right hip as a symbol of the sword of the spirit, which is the word of God. Various headpieces are worn to indicate distinctions bestowed by the bishop. A side adornment, a diamond-shaped piece worn on the right side, is another vestment of distinction. The miter is similar to a crown and serves as an emblem of the power bestowed upon an ordained priest of the church. It is also symbolic of the crown of thorns worn by the Savior.

The miter is the highest ecclesiastical award for Orthodox priests and is given for outstanding service to the Orthodox Church. It is a royal decoration given to a few archpriests because they have imitated Christ in their service to mankind. It is a symbol of authority given to outstanding workers in Christ's vineyard.

The vestments of a bishop include all of the vestments of a priest with the exception that a bishop does not wear the chasuble or the epigonation. A bishop's head covering, black in color, is draped with a monastic veil. A Metropolitan's headpiece is white with a cross inscribed on the front of it.

| Panagia (Chest Decoration) | Miter | Orletz (The Eagle) | Honorary Headpieces |

In place of a chasuble, a bishop wears a dalmatic which resembles the wide-sleeved dalmatic worn by deacons. This dalmatic is a symbolic of Christ's coat without a seam, woven from top to bottom and signifies the humbleness of a shepherd.

The stole worn by a bishop is called a pall. It is very wide and is worn over the shoulders, hanging down in front and behind over his other vestments. The pall represents the wandering sheep which Christ, the Good Shepherd, took upon His shoulders to bring to the Father. Arrayed on this vestment is the image of the Savior.

The miter, a crown-like headpiece that is beautifully decorated, is worn by a bishop to indicate the power bestowed by his ordination in the Orthodox Church and also symbolizes Christ's crown of thorns worn at His trial before His crucifixion.

A bishop wears a chest decoration—a small round or oval icon image of the Savior and the Holy Theotokos, Mother of God. It is not large but is richly decorated and is worn to remind a bishop that in his heart he must always bear the Lord and His Holy Mother. Next to this chest adornment, a bishop wears a jeweled cross.

Bishops carry a crosier, a pastoral staff which serves as a symbol of spiritual authority over their flocks, the districts they serve.

Worshippers at a Divine Service at which a bishop serves are blessed with candles. The double candleholder used is called a dikiri, representing the two natures of Christ, human and divine. The candleholder for three candles is called a trikiri, representing the Holy Trinity, Father, Son and Holy Spirit.

When a bishop serves, a small circular rug that only a bishop may stand on during the Divine Service is used. This rug, called the eagle, has an eagle soaring over a battlemented city inscribed on it. The view of the city denotes the bishop's rule over his territory and the pictured eagle represents the loftiness and purity of his teachings. The eagle rug, spread for a bishop to stand on, signifies that by his life and teachings, the bishop must emulate the eagle, soaring above earthly things and aspiring to heaven.

Deacon in vestments for assisting in celebration of the Divine Liturgy   *Bishop robed for celebration of the Divine Liturgy*   *Priest vested for celebration of the Divine Liturgy*

During His earthly mission, Christ gave the Apostles the responsibility of leading mankind to salvation. The gift of the Holy Spirit was sent to them and they were empowered to pass on this grace by laying-on of hands (ordination) of those considered worthy successors. These in turn passed the blessing to others, founding the Apostolic Succession. Every properly ordained Orthodox priest can trace a line of ordained priesthood unbroken since the original Apostles. As the Christian church grew, three ranks of Holy Orders were established: Bishops, Priests and Deacons.

7. PERSONS PERFORMING DIVINE SERVICES

In the Eastern Orthodox Church, the divine services are usually conducted by a priest who has the sanction of the Bishop. Priests conduct all services except those exclusively reserved to the higher episcopal office.

There are several different titles applied to members of the Orthodox clergy. These include protopresbyters, archimandrites, archpriests and hieromonachs. These titles indicate special distinctions for the priest or the special duties of the sacerdotal office. An archpriest is accorded the title of Very Reverend.

Usually, Bishops have jurisdiction over specified areas and have the right to perform all the sacraments. To Bishops alone is reserved the right to ordain qualified aspirants to the holy office of priesthood, the right to consecrate the holy oil (chrism) and the right to bless temples of worship.

Some Bishops are called by the title of Patriarch while others are known at Metropolitans, Archbishops and Exarchs. They are all addressed as Your Grace. A suffragan who has no independent diocese and who serves as an assistant to an elder Bishop also holds the title of Bishop.

Bishops are equal among themselves but hold rank according to their years of service. Older Bishops who have been elevated are called Archbishops and Metropolitans. Patriarch is the highest rank in the Orthodox priesthood. Deacons and priests may be married but Bishops and higher ranks must be unmarried.

Deacons help the Bishop or Priest in conducting church services and the performance of the sacraments. There are three grades in the order of deacons including archdeacon, protodiacon and hierodiacon.

In addition to the Bishops, Priests and Deacons, others who assist in the Orthodox church services include sub-deacons, readers, singers and serving boys (acolytes). None of these are ordained or included in Holy Orders but they must have the blessing of the Bishop or Priest before serving.

COLOR SYMBOLISM OF CHURCH VESTMENTS

Colored vestments are used by the Orthodox clergy in performing services. White vestments are used for most of the feasts of our Lord, the feasts honoring the Virgin Mary and feast days dedicated to the angels and saints who were not martyrs. White symbolizes joy and innocence. It also symbolizes glory.

Red vestments are used on feast days dedicated to the Holy Spirit and on special days honoring the Apostles and martyrs. Red is symbolic of the fire of divine charity. Red also is symbolic of martyrdom and the blood of the martyrs.

Green vestments are used on the Sundays after Epiphany and Pentecost. They are also worn on ordinary days when no special church feast is commemorated. Green is symbolic of the desire to attain heaven. It also denotes hope.

Purple or violet vestments are used during Advent and Lent and for vigil services. Violet is symbolic of fasting; it also denotes penance.

Black vestments are worn by the clergy on Good Friday, for services and memorials for the dead and during Lent. Black is symbolic of death and darkness. Black also denotes mourning. White, used in conjunction with black vestments, is symbolic of the hope of eternal light for all sinful souls in the darkness of hell.

To the worshiper, white reminds us that we are admonished to lead pure and holy lives. Red reminds the worshiper that we must live by divine charity and green reminds us to put our hopes of eternal life in heaven. Violet reminds us that we must do penance or atone for our sins and black gives the worshiper a tangible reminder that all must die. Black also reminds us to pray constantly for the dead.

PROPER MANNER OF ADDRESSING ORTHODOX CLERGY

Among the Bishops, the Ecumenical Patriarch (Patriarch of Constantinople —the first among equals) is addressed as His Holiness in writing or reference and as Your Holiness in direct address. Other Patriarchs, in referring to or addressing each other, use His Beatitude or Your Beatitude.

Metropolitans are addressed as His Eminence the Most Reverend Metropolitan or Your Eminence. Archbishops are addressed as The Most Reverend Archbishop or Your Eminence. Bishops are addressed as The Right Reverend Bishop in reference or writing and directly as Your Grace.

The proper manner for a clergyman or layman to greet a Metropolitan, Archbishop or Bishop is to approach him, place the right hand in the high church dignitary's left palm, and after bowing, say, "May I have your blessing, Your Grace?" When the Bishop gives the blessing and places his hand on that of the clergyman or layman, the latter kisses the Bishop's hand.

All Priests are addressed as Father. Archimandrites of the monastic order are addressed as The Right Reverend Archimandrite; Mitred Protopriests (Archpriests) as The Right Reverend; Archpriests (Protopriests) as The Very Reverend; Secular Priests as The Reverend, and Hieromonks (Priests of the monastic order) as The Reverend. In direct address, all of these are addressed as Your Reverence.

All Deacons are addressed as Father Deacon. Archdeacons (of the monastic order) or Protodeacons (married) are addressed as The Reverend Archdeacon or The Reverend Protodeacon. Deacons are addressed as The Reverend Deacon.

3

Divine Liturgy

THE DIVINE LITURGY

THE VESPER SERVICE

THE SEVEN SACRAMENTS

INCENSE AND CENSING

CHURCH BELLS – ANGELS

HOLY TRADITION – THE TRINITY

SIGN OF THE CROSS

MUSIC

STANDING, KNEELING, REVERENCING

SERVICE BOOKS

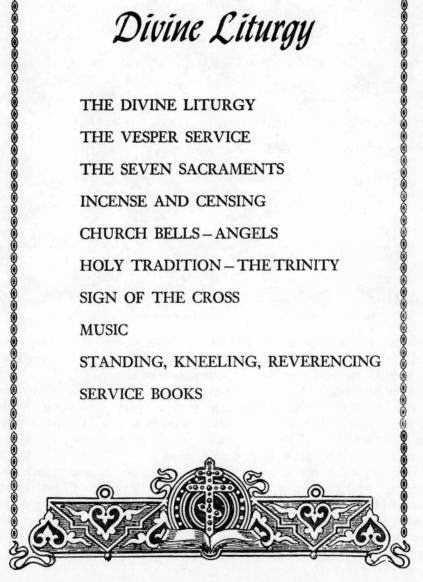

1. THE DIVINE LITURGY

The most important service in the Eastern Orthodox Church is the Divine Liturgy which was instituted by Christ just before His crucifixion, on the Thursday of the Last Supper.

When Christ's time to die was approaching, He sent two of His disciples to prepare a room where they could keep the Pascal Supper. This was the supper at which the head of the family offered the Pascal lamb to God with the entire family then partaking of this lamb together with unleavened bread and wine. On Holy Thursday, Christ and His disciples met to keep this Pascal feast now known as the Last Supper.

Ancient Tabernacle — predecessor of the modern House of Worship

During that supper, Christ and His disciples offered the Pascal lamb to God but shortly after, Christ, the true Lamb of God, was to offer Himself as a sacrifice to the Father for the redemption of sinners.

Christ performed a series of actions during this supper. To His Father He offered bread and wine, consecrated with a blessing. Blessing the bread He said, "This is My Body which shall be given to you." Over the wine He said, "This is My Blood, shed for you for the remission of sins." Thus He gave Himself to His disciples in Holy Communion.

The Divine Liturgy is accorded its importance because it includes the Sacrament of Holy Communion which was instituted by Christ. He commanded His disciples to always perform Holy Communion in His memory.

The disciples therefore instituted a prescribed ritual or Order of the Liturgy which was transmitted orally while the apostles were still alive. In this early ritual, the Liturgy of St. James was prominent.

54

In the fourth century, the liturgy was put into written form by John Chrysostom and Basil the Great. These two liturgies, and a third form instituted by St. Gregory (which is used only on certain days of the Great Lent) are the liturgies used in the Eastern Orthodox Church at the present time.

In the Divine Service, the priest follows the acts of Christ at the Last Supper. At the very beginning of the Last Supper, Christ performed a profound act of humility, washing Himself and then washing the feet of His disciples. He prayed at great length and spoke to the disciples about God and their own destiny.

The priest begins the Divine Liturgy by humbly confessing his sins at the foot of the altar and emulating Christ by washing his hands. He prays, reads from the Gospel and instructs the faithful. The priest offers a sacrifice to God with the bread and wine mystically changing into the Body and Blood of Christ.

The liturgy, with the exception of those high days of the church such as Easter and Christmas when the service begins around midnight, must be celebrated between daybreak and noon. The liturgy can be performed only by a priest or bishop and those ordained may conduct only one Divine Liturgy in one day. Likewise, only one Divine Liturgy can be performed on the same altar during a day.

The liturgy of St. John Chrysostom is used throughout the year for most Sunday services. The liturgy of St. Basil is used ten times a year (mainly on Sundays during the Great Lent) with the prayers of the priests in this liturgy differing from those in the liturgy of John Chrysostom. The liturgy of Presanctified Gifts (St. Gregory) is a Lenten period service.

MAIN PARTS OF THE DIVINE LITURGY
(St. John Chrysostom)

1. The Proskomide (Liturgy of Oblation)
2. Liturgy of the Catechumens
   The Great Litany
   The First Antiphon (Psalm 103)
   The Little Litany
   The Second Antiphon
   The Little Litany
   The Third Antiphon (The Beatitudes)
   The Little Entrance
   The Trisagion (Prayer)
   Reading of the Epistle and Gospel for the Day
   Litany of the Catechumens
3. Liturgy of the Faithful
   The Great Entrance (Hymn of the Cherubim)
   The Creed
   Sacrament of Communion
   The Lord's Prayer
   Benediction (Including Ectenia)

2. THE PROSKOMIDE

The first part of the Divine Liturgy consists of the preparation of the elements—the bread and wine—used in the Sacrament of Communion.

A custom prevailing among the early Christians was the bringing of bread and wine to the church for use during the service. From this comes Proskomide, a Greek word meaning to bring offering.

The altar bread itself which is used in the communion is called Prosphora, meaning bringing. This bread must be made from pure wheat flour, leavened, round in shape and in two layers to signify the two natures of Christ, heavenly and earthly. The Prosphora is stamped on top with a four-pointed cross which divides the loaf into four sections. Each of these sections is marked with the symbols: IC, XC, NI, KA. The first two sets of letters denote Jesus Christ and the last two pairs denote, "By this sign prevail."

Five loaves are used in the preparation for the Divine Liturgy, in token of the miraculous feeding of the five thousand by Christ. For the Sacrament of Eucharist, however, only one of the loaves is used and from it the priest lifts the Agnets (Host) with the Spear and places it on the Paten. This symbolizes the placing of Jesus in the manger at His nativity. This portion is called the Lamb, representing Christ, the Lamb of God who takes away the sins of the world.

The wine used in the sacrament must be red in color, resembling blood, and made from grapes. After the Lamb has been deposited on the Paten, it is pierced on the right side by the priest who says, "One of the soldiers did pierce His side with a spear and straightway there came forth blood and water." After the words, "blood and water" the priest pours wine and a few drops of water into the Chalice to be consecrated into the blood of Christ. The mixing of the wine and water commemorates the blood and water which flowed from the pierced side of Christ as He hung on the cross.

From the second Prosphora, a particle is taken in memory of the Virgin Mary.

Diagram showing the dedicated portions of the Prosphora (Holy Bread)

Prosphora

Nine particles are taken from the third Prosphora in commemoration of the nine ranks of glorified saints. These include: 1) The forerunner, 2) the Prophets, 3) the Apostles, 4) the Hierarchies, 5) the Martyrs, 6) the Chaste, 7) the Unmercenaries, 8) Joachim and Anna and the saints who are being commemorated on the day the Liturgy is being celebrated, 9) in honor of the originator of the Liturgy being performed, either St. John or Basil the Great.

Particles taken from the fourth loaf are for the health and salvation of the living and particles taken from the fifth Prosphora are for the remission of sins of the dead.

Having completed the preparation of the Elements, the priest places the Star-cover over the Paten, saying, "And the Star came and stood over the place where the Child was."

3. LITURGY OF THE CATECHUMENS

The second portion of the Divine Liturgy is primarily instructive in its content. In the early church the Catechumens (those being instructed in the teachings of the Christian Faith and preparing for Baptism) were permitted to be present during this part of the service.

At the beginning of the Liturgy of the Catechumens, the Antiphons are sung. These are Psalms that are so named because they are sung alternately, verse by verse. Included are the 102nd and 145th Psalms with others appropriate to the occasion sung in antiphonic manner on great festival days.

After the second antiphon, a hymn is sung and after the third antiphon the Little Entrance takes place.

The Little Entrance is accompanied by the singing of the Beatitudes (from Christ's Sermon on the Mount); it is a ceremonial procession of the Book of the Gospels. The priest, preceded by servers carrying candles, comes out through the North Door of the Sanctuary carrying the Book of the Gospels. The Little Entrance proceeds around the Holy Throne with the priest carrying the Gospel held aloft, symbolizing Christ's bringing the Word of God to the world.

In front of the Royal Doors, the priest raises the Holy Gospel, makes the sign of the cross and intones, "Wisdom! Let us attend!" He then enters the Sanctuary through the Royal Doors to replace the book on the Holy Table.

The Little Entrance symbolizes the walks of Jesus through the cities and villages of Judea with His disciples and His preaching of the Gospel of the Kingdom of God. The Little Entrance is preparatory to the reading of the Gospel to the worshipers.

The Book of the Gospels represents the very person of Christ and reminds the worshipers of the wisdom contained in the Holy Word. The lighted candles carried by the servers commemorate John the Baptist, the forerunner of Christ. The cross-wise elevation of the book in front of the Royal Doors symbolizes the victory of Christianity throughout the world.

The Trisagion hymn is then sung—the thrice-holy hymn, "Holy God,

Holy Almighty, Holy Immortal, have mercy on us. On some occasions, festive church days, the Trisagion is replaced with the singing of "All who were baptized into Christ have put on Christ, Alleluia." In early Christian times, on the eve of church festival days, baptism of catechumens was performed. Those who were to be baptized stood in the temple dressed in white garments to receive a welcome into the church.

The Epistle from the Apostle and the reading of the Gospel for the day follow. The Epistle reading is from the Book of Acts from Easter to Pentecost and from the New Testament books of the Bible called Epistles during the rest of the year.

The Gospel reading is from one of the four Gospels with each designated for a season of the year. From Easter to Pentecost, the Gospel of St. John is read, followed in turn with periods of reading from Matthew, Luke and Mark.

The sermon usually comes next, followed by the Ectenias (litanies that consist of petitions chanted by the priest or deacon with responses sung by the choir). In early Christian days, those preparing for baptism left the service at this time with only those already baptized remaining for the Liturgy of the Faithful.

4. LITURGY OF THE FAITHFUL

The Liturgy of the Faithful is the mystical portion of the Divine Liturgy for it includes the consecration of the Gifts and the Communion to the Faithful. In the ancient Church the Catechumens were not permitted to participate or to be present at this part of the service.

The important parts of this section of the liturgy includes the following: Transfer of the prepared gifts from the credence table to the Holy Table, final preparation of the faithful for the celebration of the Sacrament of Communion, performance of Communion itself and the preparation of the worshipers to receive the Holy Gifts.

During this portion of the Divine Liturgy, the elements of bread and wine are transferred to the Holy Table in a sacred procession called the Great Entrance. In this procession the priest carries the holy vessels containing the bread and wine which are to become the body and blood of Christ.

The Great Entrance commemorates the entry of Christ into His final suffering and death; His entrance into the world in the incarnation. His entrance into Jerusalem on Palm Sunday, His bearing the Cross to Golgotha, His death on the Cross and His burial in the tomb. The closing of the Royal Doors and the drawing of the curtain symbolizes the rolling of the stone in front of the tomb of Christ to seal the grave.

Following the Great Entrance, the ectenia for the precious gifts is given, followed by the singing of the Creed. During the rendering of the Creed, the priest lifts the veil which covers the elements and fans them with it from above. This symbolizes the breath of grace of the Holy Spirit, the earthquake occurring at the time of Christ's resurrection and the truth of the doctrines embodied in the Creed.

The singing of the Eucharistic Canon follows the Creed. While the choir sings, "We praise Thee, we bless Thee, we give thanks to Thee, O Lord, and we pray unto Thee, O our God," the priest invokes the Holy Spirit to sanctify the bread and wine.

During this moment, the loftiest and most sacred in the Divine Liturgy, the choir sings in soft and reverent tones. Making the sign of the Cross in a threefold invocation, the priest says, "And make this bread the precious Body of Thy Christ. And this which is the Chalice, the precious Blood of Thy Christ. Transmuting them by Thy Holy Spirit. Amen, Amen, Amen." At this moment, transubstantiation is accomplished and the bread and wine become the Body and Blood of Christ.

An ectenia begins the preparation of the faithful for partaking of the Holy Eucharist after which the Lord's Prayer is given. Communion then begins with those performing the service partaking of the Holy Gifts to signify the manner in which the disciples received Communion from Christ at the Last Supper.

The curtain is drawn aside, the Royal Doors are opened and the Holy Chalice is brought out by the priest. This symbolizes the rolling away of the stone from the Sepulchre and the Glorious Resurrection of Christ.

A prayer is read and the faithful are invited to draw near and partake of Holy Communion. After giving Communion to the faithful, the priest gives his blessing and the choir sings. The priest then takes the Chalice and blesses the worshipers with it. Then he carries the Holy Gifts to the offertory table in commemoration of Christ's Ascension into Heaven. The last showing of the Gifts to the faithful, after which they are hidden from view, represents the Ascension.

The Liturgy of the Faithful concludes with an ectenia in which the worshipers thank the Lord for His great favors and the priest responds with a prayer for the President, the clergy, the armed forces and all those who love the Lord. The dismissal benediction is then given.

LITURGY OF ST. BASIL THE GREAT

On ten occasions during the Eastern Orthodox Church year, the Liturgy of St. Basil the Great is used instead of that of John Chrysostom. These ten days include the Sundays of the Great Lent (Pre-Easter) with the exception of Palm Sunday, and Great Thursday, Great Saturday, Christmas Eve, the Lord's Baptism Day and St. Basil's Day, January 1st. In the Liturgy of St. Basil, the prayers of the priest are longer and the singing considerably slower.

LITURGY OF PRESANCTIFIED GIFTS

This Liturgy is used on Wednesdays and Fridays of the Great Lent and on the first three days of Holy Week, the week preceding Easter. St. Gregory Dialogos is considered to be the author of this Liturgy which consists of prayers, readings, psalms and hymns taken from the Evening Vesper services. Added are certain prayers and hymns from the Liturgy of the Catechumens and from the Liturgy of the Faithful. Unique in the Liturgy of Presanctified Gifts is the blessing of the faithful worshipers by the priest with a lighted candle and censer.

LITURGY OF ST. JAMES

The Liturgy of St. James the Apostle is the earliest form of Orthodox Church Liturgy. Due to its lengthy petitions, which last up to five hours, the Holy Fathers deemed it wise to abbreviate or condense the lengthy portions of this Liturgy for fear that the congregations of worshipers would grow weary and listless from the long service. Thus, the Liturgies of St. Basil and St. John Chrysostom are both abridgements from the Liturgy of St. James. This Liturgy is now used only once a year, on the date commemorating this apostle.

5. THE VESPER SERVICE

The Evening Divine Service, on ordinary days, is performed separately from the Morning Service. In such cases the Evening Service consists of the reading of the Ninth Hour and the performance of Vespers. When the Evening and Morning Services are combined, the service is called the All-Night Service.

The All-Night Service is divided into two almost equal parts. The first part pertains to the Evening Divine Service and the second part the Morning Divine Service.

Wheat, wine and oil, used during the middle of the service, are blessed during the All-Night Service. The blessing of the five loaves of bread comprises the main portion of the All-Night Divine Service.

The five loaves of bread are blessed in remembrance of the feeding of the five thousand with five small loaves by Jesus. The objects blessed are distributed to the assembled worshipers to refresh themselves during the long service.

The second part of the Vesper Service, consisting of the Morning Matins, commences with the hexapsalmos, the reading of selections from the 3rd, 37th, 62nd, 87th, 102nd and 142nd Psalms.

The great ectenia comes next, followed by the hymn (troparion) sung in honor of a festival or saint. Selections from the Psalms are then read. Following the Polyeleon, from the Greek and meaning much kindness, the Royal Doors are opened and the entire church is incensed while the choir sings verses from the 134th and 135th Psalms. Hymns are then rendered.

The reading of the Gospel follows. The worshipers bow reverently to the Risen Lord and kiss His picture. On festival days, after the reading of the Gospel, the worshipers come forward to kiss the picture and are anointed with consecrated oil.

The singing of the canon, consisting of nine hymns, comes next. Before the benediction in the Evening Vespers, the great Doxology is sung.

6. THE SEVEN SACRAMENTS

The Eastern Orthodox Church recognizes seven Sacraments. Through them the Church imparts the spiritual blessings of the Holy Spirit to believers. These holy acts, also known as the Seven Mysteries, include Baptism, Chrismation, Communion, Penance, Ordination, Matrimony and Unction with Oil.

The right to administer these sacraments was transmitted by the original Apostles to their successors, the Bishops, who in turn now transmit this right to the priests through one of the Sacraments, that of Ordination.

1. BAPTISM

In the Sacrament of Baptism, the Holy Spirit cleanses the soul of sin so that the human soul enters into a relationship with God through grace and is received into the fellowship of true believers. Those baptized receive forgiveness of original sin and are united with Christ in such a way as to receive the full benefits of His redemption. They are mysteriously reborn into a spiritual Christian life. Those who have not received the Sacrament of Baptism are not permitted to receive any of the other Sacraments of the Church.

Ordinarily, the Sacrament of Baptism is administered in church but in cases of necessity may be performed in the home. In cases of extreme necessity, a layman can administer the Sacrament of Baptism. At the time of baptism, the presence of the parents is not forbidden but customarily they are not present. The mother, however, cannot be present until forty days have elapsed since the birth of the child.

In the Baptism ceremony, the priest breathes into the face of the one being baptized three times. By this he signifies that through Baptism the breath of life has been granted, just as God breathed into the nostrils of Adam, the first man. The three times indicate the life-giving Trinity.

The priest makes the sign of the cross on the brow of the one being baptized three times to signify that by personal disgression the one baptized is separated from unbelievers. The brow is considered the center of disgression. The placing of his hand on the head of the one being baptized by the priest indicates that the newly-baptized has taken refuge in the Church.

A circle is symbolic of eternity; thus, the font is circled three times with lighted candles, the censer and songs, typifying that the newly enlightened, through Baptism, has entered into a union with Christ. This also is symbolic of future spiritual happiness.

The immersion into water during Baptism signifies burial with Christ and the lifting following immersion is symbolic of resurrection with Christ to a new life.

Since infants who are brought to be baptized cannot speak or understand the meaning of this Sacrament, Godparents are needed to answer for the child and make the promises for it. Godparents are charged with the responsibility of seeing that the child is raised as a Christian, learns the prayers of the Church, attends Sunday School and Church and goes to confession and communion. Godparents should include their Godchildren in their prayers and the Godchild should have respect for the Godparents. Male Godparents must be at least fifteen years old and female Godparents thirteen or older. Customarily, the Godparents present the child baptized with a small cross and provide the crismo, the white cloth that the child is wrapped in after receiving Baptism.

When a church layman performs this Sacrament, it is performed by pouring ordinary water on the head of the person being baptized while saying, "I baptize thee in the name of the Father, and of the Son, and of the Holy Spirit."

> "Except a man be born of water and of the Spirit, he
> cannot enter into the Kingdom of God." (John 3:5)

2. CHRISMATION

In the Eastern Orthodox Church, Chrismation or Unction with Chrism is administered at the time of Baptism. Through Chrismation, the Holy Spirit fills the soul, which has been previously emptied of sin and cleansed by Baptism, with positive powers. This Sacrament gives strength for living the new life received through being baptized.

This Sacrament, also called Confirmation and which was ordained and instituted by the original Apostles, is administered by anointing the body with a substance containing olive oil and various perfumes. The perfumes symbolize the gifts of the Holy Spirit. Olive oil is used because the priests of the Old Testament were consecrated with olive oil and its use in Chrismation signifies that the newly-baptized Christian becomes an anointed one in a royal priesthood of people belonging to God.

Chrismation is administered to the newly-baptized child in the belief that the infant needs the strength that this Sacrament imparts, especially during the early formative years of life.

". . . Ye have an unction from the Holy One, and ye know all things. And the anointing which ye have received of Him abideth in you." (I John 2:20 and 27)

3. COMMUNION

Communion, the third Sacrament, is also called the Holy Eucharist. This Sacrament was ordained by Jesus Christ when, with prayer, He broke bread and offered the chalice of wine to His disciples at the Last Supper. It is a Sacrament which perpetuates the eternal love of God through sacrifice.

In the Sacrament of Communion, at the moment of the priest's invocation, the Holy Spirit descends upon the bread and wine, which have been prepared and sanctified, and transubstantiates them into the Body and Blood of Christ. This is a transubstantiation and not a transformation because the substance becomes changed while in the form of bread and wine and remaining unchanged to the eyes.

Through this Sacrament we are spiritually fed and the Sacrament of Communion is an essential part of the third portion of the Divine Liturgy, the Liturgy of the Faithful.

"Take ye and eat. This is my Body. . . . Drink ye all of this. For this is My Blood . . . shed for many for the remission of sins."

(Matthew 26:26-28)

4. PENANCE

The fourth Sacrament is Penance, or Confession. Through this Sacrament the penitent receive forgiveness of sins committed after Baptism. Through confession the believer becomes pure in heart again before God and is healed of all spiritual illness (sin).

The Parable of the Prodigal Son gives a clear explanation of the nature and origin of sin, of true repentance, and of confession and forgiveness.

All Eastern Orthodox Christians are expected to go to confession at least once a year, especially during the Great Lenten period.

This Sacrament was instituted by Jesus Christ through His words and actions,

"Receive ye the Holy Spirit, whose sins you shall forgive, they are forgiven them; and whose sins you shall retain, they are retained."

(John 20:21-23)

5. ORDINATION

Ordination, or Holy Orders of the Priesthood, is the fifth Sacrament. In this Sacrament, the Holy Spirit gives the special grace of Orders to the priest to qualify him for ministering the Sacraments and services of the Church. This grace is given by God through the act of laying on of the hands of the

63

Apostles and their successors, the Bishops, upon the heads of those who have been instructed, examined and found worthy.

In Old Testament times, certain men were designated for church services and delegated to offer sacrifices. After Jesus had offered Himself as a sacrifice for the sins of the world, the new order of priesthood originated. Christ Himself carefully chose and trained the first Christian priests and Bishops— His Twelve Disciples.

As Christianity spread, more priests were needed and these the Apostles appointed by laying their hands on the heads of those chosen, thus handing down to them the power of the Holy Spirit. The present day Bishops and priests of Eastern Orthodox churches are part of the unbroken chain that began with Christ and the Twelve Disciples. Only Bishops can ordain priests.

In the priest's performance of the Sacraments, the human counts for practically nothing but the Grace of God, the Holy Spirit, is all important. The priest, through Ordination, becomes a servant of God and the agent through whom the real performer of the Sacraments, the Holy Spirit, works.

There are three orders of the Priesthood—Bishops, priests and deacons. The duties of those who have received the Sacrament of Ordination include:

Giving religious instruction in the Eastern Orthodox faith.

Performing Baptism and Chrismation and burial of the dead. (Thus the priest is present at the beginning and end of life.)

Visiting the sick and preparing the critically ill for death.

Celebration of the Divine Liturgy and the giving of Communion.

Hearing the confessions of the faithful.

Giving advice, help and comfort to the parishioners they serve.

Giving blessings to people and things (such as homes).

Living in such a way as to be a good example to all people.

> "Take heed therefore unto yourselves . . . to feed the Church
> of God which He hath purchased with His own blood."

(Acts 20:28)

6. MATRIMONY

Through the performance of the Sacrament of Matrimony, the Holy Spirit, by His grace, unites a man and woman into marriage for the special purpose of the growth of the Church according to the commandments of God and also for the mutual benefit and assistance of husband and wife in the work of their salvation.

Jesus Christ ratified this Sacrament. He sanctified the bond of marriage with His presence at the marriage in Cana of Galilee. The Apostle Paul, greatest of the early missionaries, referred to marriage as a great Sacrament.

Through the Sacrament of Matrimony, a grace sanctifying the married life is received. This Sacrament is consecrated by prayer as an action by which men and women are joined in a spiritual union in accordance with the institutions of the Church.

An impressive part of the Orthodox marriage ceremony is the holding of crowns above the heads of the couple being married. The crowns are symbolic of the blessings and the Grace bestowed by God upon the newly-united couple. They are also symbolic of great honor, along with the responsibilities, that attends the establishment of a new Christian family. They become a King and Queen.

The bridegroom and bride drink from a common cup of wine mixed with water to indicate that they will mutually share both the happiness and misfortunes of life. The couple hold lighted candles during the marriage ceremony to show that they pledge before God to follow the light of Truth, Jesus Christ, and that they will have their way through life lighted by the teachings of the Church.

In the exchange of rings, the bride and groom pledge to share and exchange both their spiritual and physical goods; by exchanging the rings three times they also pledge eternal love and devotion.

The couple united in matrimony join their right hands together and are led around the analoy, a small table, three times. They pledge to walk life's pathway together in the ways of Christ as symbolized by the Gospel and the Cross on the analoy.

"A man shall leave his father and mother, and shall be joined unto his wife, and they two shall be one flesh." (Ephesians 5:31-32)

7. UNCTION WITH OIL

The seventh Sacrament is Unction with Oil. In this Sacrament, the Holy Spirit comes into the believer's life in its last emergency and heals the sick. As described by the Apostle James, the purpose of the performance of this Sacrament is for the restoration of health and the remission of sins.

From the very beginnings of the Christian Church, this Sacrament was practiced and ordered by the Apostles. Unction with oil provides spiritual healing to assist the medical aid given for bodily ills. For those who are critically ill, Unction prepares Orthodox Christians for leaving this world for the better life in Heaven.

The ceremony of Unction consists of seven parts, each containing one reading from the Epistles proper to the occasion, one passage from the Gospels, and a prayer of intercession on behalf of the sick person. The anointing with oil follows.

"And anointed with oil many that were sick, and healed them."
(Mark 6:13)

Two of the seven Sacraments, Ordination and Marriage, pertain to the well-being of the entire Church. The other five Sacraments pertain to the personal life and the personal salvation of the individual believer.

Through the Sacraments, Jesus Christ transmits spiritual blessings by means of material things to the believer. All of the Sacraments are of a divine nature but in their performance there must first be a visible sign that is subject to the human senses. Prayer consecrates this sign and a priest invested with the right to perform the Sacraments carries out their performance in harmony with the established ritual.

THE CENSER

The burning of incense is an important part of every Eastern Orthodox service. The burning incense is contained in a golden vessel called the censer. To this three long chains are fastened, enabling the priest or deacon to manipulate the censer freely in any desired direction.

The censer, with the incense placed within it, symbolizes the gifts offered by the Wise Men to the Infant Jesus—gold, frankincense and myrrh.

Censing is sometimes performed before sacred icons or in front of the altar. This is done to express the desire that the prayers of the worshipers may ascend to heaven just as the sweet perfume of the incense rises heavenward.

When the priest swings the censer towards the worshipers, called censing, it expresses his prayer that God may gather up the prayers of all assembled and send His blessing down upon the worshipers and that God's love and the Grace of the Holy Spirit may envelop the souls of those in church just as the fragrant incense cloud envelops them. A little reverence should be made whenever the priest swings the censer toward the worshipers.

Incense is a mixture of fragrant tree-gum ingredients. Aaron, the High Priest of Israel in the Old Testament, burned incense in the morning and evening. This was offered as a symbol of prayer and in the New Testament the same symbolism was perpetuated.

CHURCH BELLS

Church bells summon the faithful to worship in Eastern Orthodox churches. The church bells are rung at certain progressive points in the service in order that the faithful, who for some reason are not in church, may unite in their prayers with the worshipers in the church at the solemn parts of the service. During the Divine Liturgy, the bell is rung while the Holy Gifts are being consecrated.

The church bells are rung during processionals around the church building on festive days such as Easter. In Europe, the church bells were rung every day of Easter week from sunrise to sunset with interruptions only for services. The ringing of the bells during Easter signifies the great joy brought to us by Christ's victory over death.

The church bells are also tolled to announce the death of a member of the parish. The mourning bells are tolled three times a day—morning, noon and evening (sunset)—from the time of death to the time of the burial hour.

ANGELS

Angels are invisible spirits which are usually represented with wings to indicate the speed with which they carry messages from God to man. Angels are also sometimes depicted as small children to indicate that they are without sin and that they possess eternal youth.

The number of angels is probably beyond count but only three of them—Michael, Raphael and Gabriel are known by name. The Scriptures frequently refer to multitudes of angels and there is a personal guardian angel for everyone.

In types, there is a wide variation in angels; there are nine classes or choirs of them. Included are Angels, Archangels, Princedoms, Powers, Virtues, Dominations, Thrones, Seraphim and Cherubim.

Angels are endowed with knowledge far superior to that of man; they know all things that happen on earth. They are also endowed with great strength as indicated by the angel who slew 185,000 Assyrians in the Scriptures and the ease with which the angel at the resurrection rolled away the huge stone sealing the sepulchre of Christ.

There are also evil angels who, headed by Lucifer, do the bidding of Satan.

THE HOLY TRINITY

The Eastern Orthodox Church believes in the dogma of the Holy Trinity —that God is One but that there are three Persons in God, each distinguished by personal characteristics. All three Persons of the Trinity are of one Divine Substance, are One God and are co-eternal with each other.

God the Father is characterized in that He is the Cause and Origin; God the Son is characterized as Begotten of the Father; the Holy Spirit is characterized by proceeding from the Father.

A visible resemblance to this Trinity is found in the sun. First of all, the sun is a complete globe and is the cause and origin as from it comes light which we can see and heat which we can feel.

HOLY TRADITION

The spiritual treasures that have been inherited from the ancestral Holy Fathers compose the Holy Tradition. These traditions, which are older than the Scriptures are in absolute accord with them. They are larger in extent than the Scriptures and serve to better our understanding and interpretation of the Word of God.

The Holy Tradition includes:

Short definitions and formulations of the Orthodox Creed.
The doctrine of the Seven Sacraments and the rituals for performing them.
The canons of the Apostles.
The canons of the Seven Ecumenical Councils.
The canons and regulations of the provincial synods or councils.
Disciplinary rules of Basil the Great and some of the other Saints.
Divine Liturgies and other church services.
The writings of the church Fathers.
The lives of the Christian saints and martyrs.
Signs, symbols and religious accessories used to express our faith.

Holy Tradition and Holy Scriptures are inseparable. Through Holy Tradition a better understanding of the Holy Scriptures is obtained and through the Scriptures a more complete understanding and appreciation of the Holy Tradition is made possible. The guardian of the Holy Tradition is the hierarchy of the Church.

THE SIGN OF THE CROSS

The Sign of the Cross is a part of the religious ritual that is observed by all followers of the Eastern Orthodox faith. The making of the sign (crossing ourselves) is a reverent act and is accompanied by prayer. It is a reminder that we are children of God and by making the sign of the Cross we signify our desire to serve Him.

To make the Orthodox sign of the Cross, the first three fingers of the right hand are folded together (the thumb and the two adjacent fingers) with the two remaining fingers bent downward into the palm of the hand. The three joined fingers are then touched first to the forehead, then to the chest and then to the right shoulder and to the left shoulder.

The joining of the thumb and two fingers to make the sign symbolizes the Holy Trinity—God the Father, God the Son and God the Holy Spirit and indicates a belief in the triune God.

The two fingers that are bent downward into the palm signify a belief in the two existences of Jesus Christ—as true God and also as mortal man. The two fingers indicate His heavenly and earthly existences.

The forehead is touched to make our minds and thoughts holy, the breast is touched to make our hearts pure and kind, the shoulders are touched to give our arms and hands the power to do good works. By the sign of the Cross we give our minds, our hearts and our strength to the service of God.

The right shoulder is touched first and then the left because Christ ascended into heaven and sits on the right hand of God the Father Almighty. Those saved will likewise be on the right side of God in heaven.

Symbolically, the right is always given preference over the left in the Scriptures. Christ came to minister to his own people, the Jews, who were God's chosen people and on the right hand of God. When He was rejected He turned to the Gentiles.

The making of the sign of the Cross is observed during individual prayers and at certain times during the church services. If another prayer is not recited at the time of crossing, a prayer to the Trinity should be offered: "In the name of the Father, and of the Son, and of the Holy Spirit, Amen."

Following the making of the sign of the Cross, reverence to God should be further expressed by bowing the head. Eastern Orthodox Christians cross themselves on entering the church and before kissing a holy icon. The sign of the Cross is also made at the end of every prayer and when the blessing is given by the priest.

ORTHODOX CHURCH MUSIC

Sacred music as a part of church worship dates back to the Old Testament times—to the time of King David and King Solomon. As far back as the year 900 B.C. the Temple included a special school for music students with 288 enrolled in 24 grades. The melodic idiom of early sacred music was that of the Jewish Temples and the singing of the Psalms of David is still prominent in the Eastern Orthodox Liturgy.

The music of the ancient East, where Christianity itself had its beginnings, has been lost as has been most of the music of the early Eastern Orthodox Church due to Islamic conquests and the Crusades. But the music of modern times dates its form back to the early Eastern Church culture. It is recorded that Christ and His Disciples sang a hymn after the Last Supper.

The fundamentals of music were inherited from the Near East by the Greeks and it was the Greeks who developed the theories of scales, acoustics and esthetics in the forms that are still in use. The greatest contribution from Greece, however, was choral singing. In the time of Pliny chanting in alternate chorus was popular.

In the early churches the music employed was entirely vocal. For worship, the Church Fathers were opposed to instrumental music and the tradition they established of singing "a cappella" is still followed in Eastern Orthodox churches. The priest and the choirs sing all parts of the service without accompaniment, although many Greek churches now have organs.

In the fourth century, St. Ambrose, the Bishop of Milan, blended elements of music into the church Liturgy with the New Testament and early church traditions used as the sources. Some of the Ambrosian chants (they were either very simple or very elaborate) are still well known and St. Ambrose has gained recognition in both the Eastern and Western churches as the father of church music.

During the sixth century, Gregory I, Archbishop of the then Orthodox Catholic Church of Rome, did much to stabilize the melodies and liturgical chants. The plain chant reached its zenith in his time and the entire Christian world sang Gregorian chants. His chants are still in use in the Western Church and he exerted influence on the Eastern Church.

In the eighth century, St. John of Damascus, the last of the great Greek Church Fathers, compiled the liturgical chants which are still in use. He became known as the Prince of the Hymnodists. He compiled the Ocatoechos, the book of Eight Tones, and later the melodies used were broken down into sets of eight tones. The four-line music staff was not devised until the eleventh century and the five-line music staff of modern times was devised in the seventeenth century.

Present day Eastern Orthodox Church music has developed from the early Greek background through stages which showed marked influence of Italian, Russian, German and other nationality composers. The renditions of the modern Orthodox Church choirs, singing a cappella, are beautiful and meaningful parts of the Divine Liturgy. They are the heritage of the entire history of the Eastern Orthodox Church.

STANDING, KNEELING AND REVERENCING

The proper times for Standing:
1. During the Little Entrance
2. While the Apostle text (Epistle) is being read
3. While the Gospel lesson is being read
4. During the time the Creed is sung or read

The proper times for Kneeling:
1. After arrival in church, before the service, while offering prayers
2. During the Great Entrance
3. During the singing of the Eucharistic Canon at the presentation of "Let us give thanks unto the Lord"
4. During the singing of the Lord's Prayer

The proper times for Reverencing:
A Little Reverence is made:
1. Each time the priest or deacon bows to the worshipers or blesses them
2. At each response when the choir sings, "Lord, have mercy," "Grant it, O Lord," or "To Thee, O Lord"

EASTERN ORTHODOX SERVICE BOOKS

There are twelve principal books used in services of the Orthodox church. These are divided into three groups—for use by Bishops, Priests and Deacons; for use by the Readers and the Choir; and for use by the worshiper. These books assist in following the established order of the service.

APOSTOLOS or BOOK OF EPISTLES. Contains readings from the Acts of the Apostles and Epistle readings for Sundays and Holy Days of the entire year. This book is called the Apostle because most of the readings are from the books of the Bible written by St. Paul. This book is divided into two parts— the Seasons and the Saints. The arrangement for the Seasons is in two divisions; from Easter until Pentecost the readings are from Acts and from Pentecost until Holy Saturday the readings are from the Epistles.

EVANGELION. This book contains readings from the Four Gospels, arranged in sections for reading at services. Each of the four Evangelists is read during a prescribed period of the year. St. John is read for seven weeks, from Easter to Pentecost. St. Matthew is read for eleven weeks beginning with Monday in Pentecost week, in addition to six other weeks divided between Matthew and Mark, with Matthew readings ending with the Sunday of the Exaltation of the Holy Cross. St. Luke is read for nineteen weeks, from the Monday after Exaltation of the Holy Cross until the first Sunday in Lent. From the thirteenth week on, however, only Sundays and Saturdays are reserved for Luke with readings from Mark on the remaining five days of each week during this period. The Evangelion, richly bound, usually remains on the altar in commemoration of Christ as teacher and symbolic of Christ's presence in the Sacrament.

PSALTER or PSALTERION. Contains the 150 Psalms of David arranged for recitation during the liturgy. This book is divided into twenty sections.

OKTOECHOS or PARACLETIKE. The book of eight tones. This book of supplication includes the tones for Sunday and for each day of the week. Joseph the Hymn-writer made the final arrangements of this book with a total of ninety-six canons. Each day of the week is specially commemorated: Monday is dedicated to Angels; Tuesday, St. John the Forerunner and the Prophets; Wednesday, the Holy Cross and the Virgin Mary; Thursday, the Apostles, Doctors of the church and miracle workers; Friday, the Passion, the Cross and the Crucifixion; Saturday, Saints, Martyrs and departed souls; and Sunday, the Resurrection. The book of tones is used during the entire year except for periods when the Triodion or the Pentecostarion is used.

TRIODION. The name of this book is derived from the fact that most of the Canons have only three Odes instead of nine. The Triodion is used for services for the ten weeks preceding Easter, including the four weeks before the Great Lent and the ritual for Holy Week. This period begins with the Sunday of the Pharisee and the Publican and ends with Holy Saturday.

PENTECOSTARION. This book gives the service from Easter to the Sunday after Pentecost.

MENAIA. The Service of the Saints. A collection of twelve books, one for each month of the year. These twelve volumes include services for all feasts with fixed dates, arranged from September first, the beginning of the church year, to August 31st. The Menaia also includes services for all holy days honoring the Virgin Mary. The order of presentation includes: Mention of the saint honored; text, mainly the canon; nine Odes, with historical notes inserted between the sixth and seventh Odes; historical notes; and finally, an invocation of God to save us through the saint's intercession. The Menaia also comes in two volumes with one devoted to canons for Great Feasts and the other to canons common for the Saints.

HOROLOGION or OGOLOGION. The Book of Hours. A prayer book containing all the services read during the day with related prayers and hymns of the day. Includes a listing of saints commemorated during the year and intercession canons to the Virgin Mary, the Holy Cross and the Angels. Also includes Troparions for Sunday and week days.

EUCHOLOGION. The Book of Needs. Contains the complete texts for the Seven Sacraments and sacramental services of the church. Also includes monastic ritual, ritual for the dead, consecration rituals for churches and holy objects, blessing of homes, and other blessings and ceremonies along with various prayers for special occasions.

TYPIKON. A book of formularies regulating detailed services for every day of the year. This is a calendar-type book guiding the clergy and chanters for all occasions. The Typikon includes regulations concerning fast days and tables of the fixed feasts.

LITURGIKI. The priest's guide. This book gives the texts of the liturgies of St. John Chrysostom, St. Basil and the Liturgy of Pre-Sanctified Gifts. The Liturgiki also contains an abridgment of sacramental rituals (the Seven Sacraments).

HEIRMOLOGION. This book contains those parts of the service usually sung by the choir. Its origin goes back to the time when the Canons were no longer sung in their entirety, with the greater part of the Troparia read and only the Heirmos of each ode sung.

4

Easter

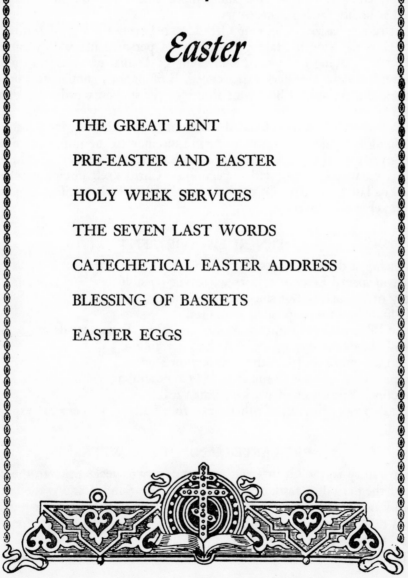

THE GREAT LENT

Of the four Lenten periods during the Orthodox Church year the most important is the GREAT LENT, a seven weeks period prior to Easter. Actually, this Great Lent is divided into two parts. The first forty days commemorate the forty days and forty nights that Christ fasted in the Jordan desert before beginning His ministry. The week before Easter, called Holy Week or Passion Week, commemorates the suffering and death of Christ.

Lent is a period of self-denial and self-examination. The word Lent itself means spare, plain, or meager, and means abstinence from food. The purpose of fasting is to instill in the Orthodox believer a greater refinement of purpose, an increased sensitivity to God and a more chaste outlook on life. Spiritual as well as bodily fasting is necessary.

Lent re-emphasizes to all true Orthodox believers the true depth of faith. It is a time set aside for taking inventory of personal life with changes for the better replacing recognized shortcomings. Denial of pleasures should be made and sincere sacrifices experienced. Tribulations should be borne patiently and there should be a watchfulness over spoken words, thoughts and deeds.

Lent is a period for accentuated works of mercy and charity. Visiting the sick, doing helpful deeds for others and assistance to the unfortunate should all be given special consideration during this time. The believer should adhere to a stricter way of living with reflection on Christ's self-discipline when He spent His last forty days on earth before his trial and crucifixion in fasting and prayer in the desert.

TEN RULES FOR LENT

Worship at divine services every Sunday.
Attend special Lenten services whenever possible.
Pray often—briefly but sincerely.
Meditate often on dependence on God.
Read Bible passages from the Psalms and New Testament daily.
Read one or more religious books or biographies.
Use moderation in food, drink and entertainment.
Prepare carefully for Confession and Communion.
Practice Christian charity with greater zeal.
Refrain from criticism of others and from boasting of personal exploits.

PRE-EASTER AND HOLY WEEK

Preparatory to the Great Lent, the Sunday two weeks prior to the beginning of the period of fasting is called Meat Fare Sunday and is the last time before Easter that meat is eaten. The Sunday a week before the beginning of Lent is called Cheese Fare Sunday and is the last day before Easter on which cheese, butter and milk are eaten.

The first Sunday of the Great Lent is observed as Orthodox Sunday and is dedicated to the victory of Orthodoxy. The second Sunday is dedicated to the Archbishop of Salonica, Gregory Palamas. The third Sunday of the Great Lent is observed as the Sunday of the Adoration of the Cross and is dedicated to the liberation of the Holy Cross from the Persians by the Byzantine King Heraklios. The fourth Sunday is dedicated to St. John, the author of Climax, and the fifth is dedicated to St. Mary of Egypt.

Palm Sunday, also known as Willow Sunday or Blooming Sunday, is one of the twelve great feast days of the Orthodox year and is dedicated to the triumphal entry of Jesus into Jerusalem.

HOLY WEEK

The final week before the observance of Christ's Resurrection is known as the Holy Week or Passion Week. These are the holiest days of the year, a time for accentuated prayer and fasting.

On the evening of Holy Thursday, the faithful gather in the church to hear the account of our Lord's Passion read from the Holy Gospel. This recitation is divided into twelve sections, each of them followed by the singing of hymns and the ringing of bells. This service, recounting all of the events of Christ's last days on earth, is called the Service of the Twelve Gospels. The faithful hold candles during this service which symbolize Christ's light eternal which came to earth to show believers the way to salvation.

Through the reading of the Twelve Gospels, we relive the trial, crucifixion, suffering and death of Christ. We see Him betrayed by Judas with a kiss, follow Him as He is led away to trial and see Him standing before the Sanhedrin, accused of blasphemy when questioned by Caiaphas, the High Priest.

We see Him spat upon, beaten and buffeted. We see Him, sadly, denied three times by Peter and brought again before Pilate. We see the thief, Barabbas, released and the people demanding Christ's crucifixion while Pilate washes his hands in weak protest.

We see Christ adorned with a scarlet cloak and a crown of thorns with the soldiers mocking Him. He is led away to stagger under the burden of the heavy Cross—and we watch Simon the Cyrene bear the Cross part of the way to Golgotha.

We see the Saviour crucified, hung on a Cross between two thieves. We see the soldiers casting lots for His robe. We see the inscription above Him, "The King of the Jews," written in three languages. We see one robber mock Him and the other repenting and promised Paradise by Christ.

We see Christ commit His mother's care to the disciple John. We see the soldier pierce His side and later Joseph of Arimathea asking for the body. We see His body tenderly anointed, wrapped in linen and buried in a new tomb. All of these events in the last days of Christ, experienced through the reading of the Twelve Gospels, lead up to and prepare us for the glorious Resurrection.

GOOD FRIDAY

Good Friday is such a great day of sorrow in the Eastern Orthodox Church that it is the only day of the year when the Divine Liturgy may not be celebrated. Afternoon services are held on this day, at three or at four in the afternoon. After this service a dark, replica tomb is brought from the altar and placed in the center of the church. The Holy Shroud, representing the robe that Christ wore at His crucifixion and bearing His image, is carried around the church and then placed in the sepulchre to signify the burial of Christ. The faithful file past this symbolic tomb, which is decked with palms and flowers, to kiss the symbolic wounds of the Saviour. Praises are sung in honor of Christ during the evening service, which is called the Lamentations.

EASTER

Easter, the most glorious and radiant event in all history, commemorates the Resurrection of Christ. Easter is the Feast of Feasts, the Triumph of Triumphs and in the Orthodox Church it is not listed among the Twelve Great Festivals as it stands above them all.

On Holy Saturday (Easter eve), the Book of Acts is read at the grave of the Lord and just as a watch was set over the tomb of the Saviour, the priest stands before the Sepulchre. This marks the last intense waiting for the announcement that Christ has risen.

With the ringing of the church bells at midnight of Saturday, the joyful

Easter Matins begin. The Royal Doors of the Sanctuary open and the priests and other clergy come forth arrayed in brilliant vestments, carrying censers and candles. Crosses, banners, the icon of the Resurrection, the book of the Gospels and the Artos (Easter Bread) are carried by the faithful.

This triumphant Resurrection service, which extends for two hours or longer, begins with a procession around the church. Temporarily the darkened church is emptied and the doors are closed, representing the closed tomb of Christ.

Singing the processional hymn, the procession circles the church three times, symbolizing the journey of the myrrh-bearing women (Mary Magdalene, Salome and Mary Cleophas) to the tomb of Christ in the early hours of the morning to anoint His body. After circling the church three times, the procession stops outside the closed doors of the empty church.

The Resurrection

The visit to the empty Sepulchre by the myrrh-bearing women was climaxed when the Risen Saviour was seen and recognized. Here the priest greets the worshipers with the traditional words, "Christ Is Risen." The people respond with, "He is indeed Risen." The church bells peal, the worshipers re-enter the church and the Easter service proceeds to its joyful completion.

All through the service the church bells peal at intervals, each clarion appeal announcing a progressive phase of the Easter worship. Special Easter music is rendered by the choir, including canticles, antiphons and other Easter music long identified with Eastern Orthodox Easter observances. The Royal Doors are kept open the entire Easter Week to symbolize that the Gates of Heaven have been opened to all faithful believers.

ARTOS

During Easter Week a loaf of bread, representing the Bread of Eternal Life and called Artos, is placed under the Icon of Christ. The custom of having this bread in church on Easter dates back to the time of the first Apostles who always left an empty place at the head of the table to honor the memory of Christ. It was their firm belief that He was invisibly present with them.

The Artos is kept on the lectern during Easter week. On St. Thomas Sunday, the eighth day after Easter, the Artos is again blessed by the priest and is then broken up and given to the worshipers.

During the period between Easter and Pentecost, because of the glory bestowed on mortals by Christ's victory over death, Orthodox Christians do not kneel in church.

TROPARION
Christ is risen from the dead, trampling down death by death, and upon those in the tomb bestowing life.

KONDAKION
Though Thou didst descend into the grave, O Deathless One, yet didst Thou annihilate the power of hell, and didst rise again as conqueror, O Christ-God, announcing unto the myrrh-bearing women: Rejoice! And giving peace unto Thine Apostles, and bestowing Resurrection upon the fallen.

78

HOLY WEEK SERVICES

HOLY MONDAY—Morning Service—Liturgy of Presanctified Gifts

HOLY TUESDAY—Morning Service—Liturgy of Presanctified Gifts

HOLY WEDNESDAY—Dedicated to the treachery of Judas
Morning Service—Liturgy of Presanctified Gifts
Evening Matins Service

HOLY THURSDAY—Dedicated to the Last Supper (Morning)
Dedicated to the Crucifixion (Evening)
Morning Service—Liturgy of St. Basil the Great
Evening Matins—Reading of the Twelve Gospels

HOLY FRIDAY—(GOOD FRIDAY) Dedicated to the death and burial of Christ
Afternoon Vesper Service
Placing of the Tomb of Christ in the center of the church
Evening Matins—Commemoration of the burial of Christ with a procession of the Tomb of Christ around the church building

HOLY SATURDAY—Dedicated to the descent of Christ into Hades
Morning Service—Liturgy of St. Basil the Great
Pre-Midnight Service
Midnight Service—Procession around the church building followed by Easter Matins and Blessing of Baskets

EASTER SUNDAY—Dedicated to the Resurrection of Christ
Morning Liturgy
Afternoon Vespers—Procession around the church building

EASTER MONDAY
and
EASTER TUESDAY
Morning Services preceded by Easter Matins
Evening Easter Vesper Service

The Last Supper

THE SEVEN LAST WORDS

During the Easter season, the Seven Last Words of Christ are remembered in sermons and as the theme of a famous choral cantata rendered by choirs.

1. "Father, forgive them, for they know not what they do." Spoken by Christ at the time he was being crucified and the Roman soldiers were casting lots for His robe. (Luke 23:34)

2. "Verily, I say unto thee, today thou shalt be with Me in paradise." Spoken to the repentant thief who hung on a cross beside Christ. (Luke 34:43)

3. "Woman, Behold thy Son! . . . Behold thy mother." Spoken to His mother and to the disciple John who was charged with taking care of Christ's mother. (John 19:26-27)

4. "My God, My God, Why hast Thou forsaken Me." Spoken by Christ during His agony on the Cross. (Matthew 27:46 and Mark 15:34)

5. "I thirst." Spoken by Christ on the Cross in His final hour. Vinegar on a sponge was administered to Him at that time. (John 19:28)

6. "Father, Into Thy hands I commend My spirit." Spoken by Christ just before His death after six hours of crucifixion. (Luke 23:46)

7. "It is finished." The final words of Christ as He died on the Cross. (John 19:30)

THE CATECHETICAL EASTER ADDRESS OF
ST. JOHN CHRYSOSTOM
(Read at the Midnight Easter Service)

If any man be devout and loveth God, let him enjoy this fair and radiant triumphal feast.

If any man be a wise servant, let him rejoicing enter into the joy of his Lord.

If any have labored long in fasting, let him now receive his recompense.

If any have wrought from the first hour, let him today receive his just reward.

If any have come at the third hour, let him with thankfulness keep the feast.

If any have arrived at the sixth hour, let him have no misgivings; because he shall in nowise be deprived therefor.

If any have delayed until the ninth hour, let him draw near fearing nothing.

If any have tarried until the eleventh hour, let him, also, be not alarmed at his tardiness; for the Lord, who is jealous of His honor, will accept the last even as the first; and to the one He giveth, and upon the other He bestoweth gifts.

And He both accepteth the deeds and welcometh the intention, and honoreth the acts and praiseth the offering. He giveth rest unto him who cometh even at the eleventh hour, even as unto him who wrought from the first hour.

Wherefore, enter ye all into the joy of your Lord; and receive ye your reward, both the first, and likewise the second.

Ye rich and poor together, hold ye high festival!

Ye sober and ye heedless, honor ye the day!

Rejoice today, both ye who have fasted and ye who have disregarded the fast.

The table is full-laden; feast ye all sumptuously! The calf is fatted; let no one go hungry away. Enjoy ye all the feast of faith. Receive ye all the riches of loving kindness.

Let no one bewail his poverty, for the universal kingdom hath been revealed.

Let no one weep for his iniquities, for pardon hath shown forth from the grave.

Let no one fear death, for the Saviour's death hath set us free. He that was held prisoner of it, hath annihilated it.

By descending into Hell, He made Hell captive. He angered it when it tasted of His flesh.

And Isaiah, foretelling this, did cry: Hell, said he, was angered, for it was overthrown. It was angered, for it was fettered in chains. It was angered, when it encountered thee in the lower regions. It was angered for it was abolished. It was angered for it was mocked. It was angered for it was slain. It was angered for it was overthrown.

81

It took a body and met God face to face.

It took earth, and encountered heaven.

It took that which was seen, and fell upon the unseen.

O death, where is thy sting?

O Hell, where is thy victory? Christ is Risen, and thou are overthrown.

Christ is Risen, and the demons are fallen.

Christ is Risen, and the angels rejoice.

Christ is Risen, and life reigneth.

Christ is Risen, and not one dead remaineth in the grave. For Christ, being risen from the dead, is become the first fruits of those who have fallen asleep.

To Him be glory and dominion unto ages and ages. Amen.

BLESSING OF BASKETS

A colorful Easter custom observed in the Eastern Orthodox Church is the blessing of Easter baskets. Each family prepares a basket which contains all the essentials for a family repast (special golden-colored bread, decorated Easter eggs, ham, sausage, butter and special foods such as an egg cheese) which is brought to the church for the Saturday midnight service. A lighted candle is placed in each basket. At the conclusion of the service and after the blessing ceremony, the baskets are taken home where the families gather for an early morning meal. These baskets represent a humble offering brought to the Resurrected Christ.

EASTER EGGS

A custom that is sometimes observed among those of the Orthodox faith is the presenting of red colored eggs to friends while giving Easter greetings. This custom had its beginning with Mary Magdalene. After the Ascension of Christ, she went to the Emperor of Rome and greeted him with, "Christ is Risen," as she gave him a red egg. She then began preaching Christianity to him. The egg is symbolic of the grave and life renewed by breaking out of it. The red symbolizes the blood of Christ redeeming the world, represented by the egg, and our regeneration through the blood shed for us by Christ. The egg itself is a symbol of the Resurrection—while being dormant it contains a new life sealed within it.

5

Great Feasts

THE LORD'S ASCENSION

THE PENTECOST

TRANSFIGURATION

ASSUMPTION OF VIRGIN MARY

NATIVITY OF VIRGIN MARY

ELEVATION OF THE CROSS

PRESENTATION TO THE TEMPLE

NATIVITY OF THE SAVIOUR

EPIPHANY

MEETING THE LORD IN THE TEMPLE

ANNUNCIATION OF THE VIRGIN MARY

ENTRY INTO JERUSALEM

LESSER FEAST DAYS

ASCENSION OF THE LORD

On the fortieth day after His Resurrection from the dead, Christ made His last appearance on earth. This final appearance was made before all of His disciples as they were gathered in Jerusalem with the Virgin Mary.

At this last appearance, Christ commanded His disciples to remain in Jerusalem for ten days—until the Holy Spirit should descend upon them. He then led the disciples to the Mount of Olives where He said to them, "All power is given Me in heaven and on earth. Go into the whole world and preach the Gospel to all nations, baptizing them in the name of the Father, and of the Son, and of the Holy Spirit. And, behold, I am with you always, even to the end of the world."

Having given this mission to the disciples, Jesus lifted up His hands and blessed the group. Then, rising slowly from the earth, He ascended into heaven to take His place through all time at the right hand of God, the Father.

In great wonderment these faithful followers continued to watch Jesus as He ascended until a cloud finally hid Him from view.

As the disciples watched, still gazing heavenward, two angels dressed in white robes appeared to them and said, "Ye men of Galilee, why stand ye gazing up into heaven? This same Jesus, which is taken up from you into heaven, shall so come in like manner as you have seen Him go into heaven." Thus, as recorded in the first chapter of the book of Acts, the world was given the promise of Christ's second coming to earth. Hearing this message from the angels, the disciples fell upon the ground and worshiped God.

Obedient to the command of the Master, the Apostles remained in Jerusalem to await the coming of the Holy Spirit. They spent their time in an upper room in prayer and holy meditation. The Virgin Mary and many other followers of Christ met with them and the assembled group numbered about a hundred and twenty.

It was during this ten-day period of waiting that Peter suggested the selection of a new twelfth disciple to replace Judas Iscariot, the disciple who betrayed Christ and who committed suicide by hanging himself after his treachery. Two followers were put forward as candidates, Joseph and Matthias, and after prayer, Matthias was chosen.

The feast day of the Ascension of Christ into heaven is observed forty days after Easter and always falls on a Thursday.

TROPARION

Thou has ascended in glory, O Christ our God, having made joyful Thy disciples by the promise of the Holy Spirit, which was announced unto them in the blessing; for Thou art the Son of God, the Redeemer of the World.

KONDAKION

When Thou hadst accomplished Thy dispensation concerning us, and united those on the earth with the heavenly, Thou didst ascend in glory, O Christ our God, yet in nowise separating Thyself from us, but abiding ever present and crying out unto those that love Thee: I am with you, and none shall prevail against you.

PENTECOST—DESCENT OF THE HOLY SPIRIT

Fifty days after Christ's Resurrection, the disciples were gathered in their upper room. At nine o'clock in the morning a sound like a great wind coming from heaven filled the room. At the same time, cloven tongues of fire appeared and settled upon each of the disciples and on the Virgin Mary. Then, as promised by the angels at Christ's Ascension, they were filled with the Holy Spirit.

Transformed by the descent of the Holy Spirit upon them, the disciples were enlightened and remembered all of the teachings of the Master during His days on earth. These teachings appeared in a new light to them and they were no longer timid or afraid as they went forth to preach the gospel of Christ.

It was during this time that the Hebrew people from all parts of the then-known world had journeyed to Jerusalem to celebrate the Jewish Pentecost. This day commemorated the receiving of the Ten Commandments by Moses on Mt. Sinai and is observed fifty days after the Jewish Passover. These travelers, speaking many varied languages, filled the streets of the city. The news of the experience of the disciples spread rapidly and in a short time a large crowd had gathered outside of the house where the Apostles were staying.

As the crowd waited in anticipation, a group of men who were readily recognized as Galileans from their mannerisms and the type of clothing they wore, came out and began to preach to the crowd. To the astonishment of all, each of those in the assembled crowd heard the Apostles speaking in his own language. Amazed at this, they began to ask, "Are not these who speak to us Galileans? How is it then that each of us hears his own native tongue?"

Some scoffers answered these queries with the declaration that the disciples were intoxicated with new wine.

Peter then arose and, standing with the eleven other disciples, he said to those assembled, "Men of Judea, and all of you that dwell in Jerusalem, know that these men are not drunk but in them the words of the prophet Joel are fulfilled."

After hearing a great sermon preached by Peter, the crowd was touched with remorse for wrong-doing and some among them asked what they should do. "Repent and be baptized in the name of Jesus Christ, for the remission of sins and you shall receive the gift of the Holy Spirit," they were told.

The feast day of Pentecost, observed by Eastern Orthodox Christians in honor of the Holy Trinity, is one of the twelve most important Holy Days of the Orthodox Church year and is commemorated fifty days after the Resurrection of Christ from the dead (Easter) and ten days after the Ascension of Jesus into heaven.

TROPARION

Blessed art Thou, O Christ our God, Who didst give wisdom to Thy fishers by sending upon them the Holy Spirit, and through them having caught the universe, O Thou who lovest mankind, Glory to Thee.

KONDAKION

When the Most High descended, He blended the tongues, dividing the nations; but when He distributed the tongues of fire, He called all into unity; Wherefore, with one accord, we glorify the All Holy Spirit.

THE TRANSFIGURATION

Jesus told His disciples on one occasion that some among them would not die until they had seen the Kingdom of God (he was in His early thirties when the time came for Him to make His last journey to Jerusalem).

About eight days after He had spoken these words, Christ took three of the disciples—Peter, James and John—up to a high mountain called Mount Hermon. They went there to pray but after the long climb the Apostles were tired and in their weariness they fell asleep.

As Jesus prayed His countenance changed and His clothing became a glimmering white. He was thus transfigured into a heavenly form and two men appeared and talked with Him. They were Moses and Elijah and they talked with Christ concerning His approaching death.

The glorious light of radiance which shown around the transfigured Christ awakened the sleeping disciples. They saw Jesus talking to the two Old Testament prophets. Awe-stricken at the great event they were witnessing, the disciples were at a loss for words. Finally, Peter said, "Lord, it is good for us to be here."

While Peter was speaking, a cloud descended upon the disciples and overshadowed them and a voice came out of the cloud saying, "This is My Beloved Son: Hear Him." When the voice had finished speaking, the three disciples found themselves alone again with Jesus.

The three disciples and Jesus then began their journey back down the mountain. Along the way, Jesus told the disciples that they should not tell anyone about the transfiguration they had witnessed until after the time when Christ had arisen from the dead.

The witnessing of the transfiguration by the three selected disciples was a fulfillment of the promise made by Jesus that some of His followers would see the Glory of the Kingdom of God before their death. He permitted the three to listen while He spoke to the prophets, Moses and Elijah, about His coming crucifixion. They also heard the voice of God.

The three disciples were strengthened in their faith to face with courage the days of Christ's torture and death that were coming in the near future. In permitting the three disciples to witness the transfiguration, Christ gave them a glimpse of the Heavenly Glory and the life that is to come.

Moses as the lawgiver and Elijah as the wonder worker were considered the greatest men of the Old Testament, but by surpassing them in glory, Christ showed that He was greater than either of them in heavenly majesty.

The Transfiguration is observed in the Eastern Orthodox Church as one of the twelve most important feast days. It is celebrated each year on August 19th with the worshipers customarily bringing fruits to the Church to be blessed.

In times past, when most people raised their own food and had their own orchards, it was customary to not eat the fruits of the orchard until the feast day of the Transfiguration when the first fruit to ripen had been blessed in Church.

TROPARION

Thou wast transfigured on the mount, O Christ our God, revealing unto Thy disciples Thy glory in so far as they could bear it. Let Thine everlasting light shine also upon us sinners, through the prayers of the Birth-giver of God. O Light-giver, Glory to Thee.

KONDAKION

Upon the mount was Thou transfigured, and Thy disciples in so far as they were capable, beheld Thy glory, O Christ our God! that when they should see Thee crucified they might therefore understand Thy passion to be voluntary and proclaim to the world that Thou verily are the effulgence of the Father.

ASSUMPTION (FALLING ASLEEP) OF THE VIRGIN MARY

Shortly after Pentecost and the Descent of the Holy Spirit, the disciples separated and went forth to preach the Gospel in many lands, carrying out the instructions given them by the Master.

The Virgin Mary remained in Jerusalem along with John, the beloved disciple who had been instructed by Jesus to take care of her. During her life the Virgin Mary preached and taught the Word of God and ministered to the sick and the poor. Christians from many far away places came to seek peace and consolation from her. On many occasions she also went to pray at the places where Christ had lived and the places where He suffered, died on the Cross, was buried and arose from the grave.

The years passed and finally Mary, the Mother of God, was nearing the end of her years on earth. Three days before her death, she was visited by the Archangel Gabriel who told her that the time for her departure from the world was near. Gabriel appeared to her with a branch of a tree from Paradise in his hand.

During this time the Virgin Mary expressed a desire to see all of the disciples before she died. With the exception of Thomas, who could not be reached, all of the disciples gathered in Jerusalem.

On the day appointed for her death in the summons from the Archangel Gabriel, the Holy Virgin prepared and ready to die, lay down on her bed. The disciples and other friends gathered around her, praying and holding lighted candles in their hands.

At about three o'clock in the afternoon, the burning candles were suddenly dimmed by blinding rays of light which completely encompassed the room. Just as suddenly, Jesus appeared in the midst of those assembled. Mary, the Mother of God, peacefully and as if she were falling asleep, then gave up her spirit.

Before her death, the Virgin Mary had selected and pointed out to the Apostles the tomb in the Garden of Gethsemane where she was to be buried. Her funeral procession was followed by large crowds and many miracles accompanied her burial.

The Jewish leaders and priests, who opposed the New Testament teachings of Christ and His followers, tried to disperse the crowds but were unsuccessful. One of the Jewish priests, Athonius, seized the body of the Holy Theotokos and tried to upset it. His hands were cut off by an invisible angel who followed the body. Athonius repented and the Apostle Peter healed him immediately.

When the disciple Thomas returned to Jerusalem three days after the burial of Mary, he was deeply grieved at having been absent during this time. To console him, the other disciples took Thomas to her tomb and removed the stone sealing the entrance. To their astonishment, the body of the Holy Virgin was not in the tomb.

Bewildered, the disciples remained at the empty grave until nightfall. They prayed continually, asking God that they might be enlightened.

Later in the evening, as they broke bread in their customary manner, the disciples beheld the Virgin Mary hovering in the air above them. She said to them, "Rejoice, I am with you always." From that time on, the disciples made it an established custom during meals to lift up the bread and say the prayer, "Most Holy Birthgiver of God, Save Us!"

The occasion of the death of the Virgin Mary is observed in the Eastern Orthodox Church on the feast day called the Assumption (Falling Asleep) of the Virgin Mary and is celebrated each year on August 28.

While the relics of many saints remain on earth, no relics remain of the Holy Virgin since her body was taken up into heaven. Her blessings and help are still available to us and we may appeal to her for assistance when in sorrow or need. The Virgin Mary is pictured on many icons and many miracles have been attributed to icons commemorating her.

TROPARION

In birth-giving thou didst preserve thy virginity, in thy falling asleep thou hast not forsaken the world, O Birth-giver of God: Thou hast passed away into life, thou who are the Mother of Life, and by thy prayers thou deliverest our souls from death.

KONDAKION

The Theotokos sleepeth not in her intercessions and she is the unfailing hope of protection. The grave and death could not retain her; for, He that dwelt in her ever-virginal womb hath presented her, as the Mother of Life, unto life.

NATIVITY OF THE VIRGIN MARY

As far back as the time of Adam and Eve, God had promised a Redeemer for mankind. When the first man and woman sinned by eating of the fruit of the Tree of Knowledge after being tempted by the serpent and were driven from the Garden of Eden, God foretold that a woman would crush the serpent's head, overcoming Satan's power.

God had also told Abraham that all of the nations of the world would be blessed through him and Jacob foretold that from the tribe of Judah among the children of Israel, one of the descendants of David would be the Saviour.

The prophets among the Israelites taught the people to keep the Commandments and told of the coming of the Messiah. Many of the nations of the world had turned away from the one true God and worshiped idols. Some Israelites believed that the Messiah would appear as a powerful earthly king who would free the Israelites from the oppression of the Romans. Some few believed in the coming of the true Messiah who would free mankind from sin and save their souls.

A childless couple, Joachim and Anna, who were descendants of King David, lived in the small town of Nazareth in Palestine. Among the Israelites, couples who had no children were believed to be punished for their sins in that way. Joachim and his wife Anna were very unhappy because they had no children but they never complained against the Lord and they prayed continually that a child would be born to them.

Joachim, following his usual practice, went up on the mountain to pray and Anna strolled in her garden. There she noticed a nest of young birds in a tree and being thus reminded of her own grief at being childless, she burst into tears. She then began to pray fervently and made a solemn promise that if God would grant her wish to have a child, the child would be dedicated to the service of the Lord.

Joachim and Anna were both God-fearing persons and Anna's prayers were answered. A daughter was born to them and they named the child Mary, meaning "Sovereign Lady."

The birth of Mary, who was to become the mother of Jesus, is one of the twelve important feast days of the Eastern Orthodox Church. This day is commemorated as the Nativity of the Virgin Mary and is observed each year on September 21st.

TROPARION

Thy nativity, O Mother of God and Virgin, hath proclaimed joy unto all the universe; for from thee is risen the Sun of Righteousness, Christ our God, and having destroyed the curse, He hath given a blessing, and having frustrated death, He hath granted us life eternal.

KONDAKION

Joachim and Anna were freed from the reproach of childlessness and Adam and Eve from the corruption of death in thy Holy Nativity, O All-pure One. This do thy people celebrate, also being redeemed from the guilt of transgressions, when they cry unto thee: The barren bringeth forth the Birth-giver of God and the Nourisher of our life.

ELEVATION OF THE PRECIOUS AND LIFE-GIVING CROSS

During the first three centuries following the crucifixion of Christ, Christianity underwent many periods of cruel persecution. Many of those who followed the new faith became martyrs. Nevertheless, Christianity spread to all areas of the world and those who became followers of the teachings of Christ included the weak and the powerful, the poor and the rich.

When Constantine the Great became the ruler of the Roman empire in 307 A.D., his right to the throne was challenged by another Roman ruler named Maxentius. They met in battle in 312 near Milvian bridge on the Tiber river after Constantine had made a surprise crossing of the Alps. On the eve of this crucial battle, with Maxentius possessing forces superior in number, Constantine was greatly worried.

Just before sunset, a miracle appeared in the sky. Beneath the sun there appeared a cross formed of bright, vivid stars with the inscription in Greek blazoned on it which said, "By This, Conquer!" The sight was amazing to behold but Constantine was unable to understand its significance.

While he was asleep that night, the Lord appeared to Constantine in a vision. He was commanded to make a banner with the sign of the Cross inscribed on it similar to the vision he had seen in the sunset skies. Overcome with elation, Constantine immediately ordered the banner to be designed. It was called "Labarum" and the sign of the Cross was inscribed on it.

In the battle which followed, Maxentius was killed and his forces were defeated. Constantine entered Rome in triumph and was proclaimed Emperor of the entire Roman empire. With this great military victory, persecution of the Christians came to an end through the Edict of Milan issued in 313 A.D. The First Ecumenical Council was convened during his time and Constantine was baptized as a Christian on his deathbed.

After he became the supreme ruler of the Roman empire, Constantine had a burning desire to discover the whereabouts of the Precious Cross. He dispatched his mother, St. Helena, to Jerusalem to institute a search for the Cross upon which Christ had been crucified. She arrived in the Holy City, made many inquiries, and finally found an aged Jew who knew where the Cross of Christ had been hidden. It had been buried in a certain hillock with a pagan temple later erected over it.

St. Helena ordered the destruction of the pagan temple and directed that the ground under it be dug up. This was done and the Cross of Christ was found but with it were the other two crosses—those used to crucify the thieves on either side of Christ.

The board with the inscription, "Jesus of Nazareth, the King of the Jews," also lay among the three crosses. Neither St. Helena nor any of the others present knew which of the three crosses was the one which had been used to crucify the Saviour. She was not to be denied, however, and had an ailing woman brought to the place. The sick woman was told to kiss each of the three crosses.

The sick woman kissed the first cross with no result. She kissed the second cross and again nothing happened. However, when the ailing woman kissed the third Cross she was immediately made well. To further ascertain that this was the true Cross, a corpse was brought to the spot and laid in turn on each of the crosses. When the body was placed on the third Cross the corpse came to life again.

St. Helena and the clergy accompanying her then acknowledged this Cross to be the Precious and Life-giving Cross of the Saviour—the one used for Christ's crucifixion—and they fell to the ground and reverenced it.

There were so many persons present at this momentous occasion that many of them could not come to the Cross and many of them could not even see it. The Patriarch of Jerusalem, Macarius, who was with St. Helena, ascended a high knoll and began to raise the Cross aloft so that all of those present could see it. In unison, the people cried out, "Kyrie eleison!" meaning, "Lord, have mercy!"

This important feast day of the Eastern Orthodox Church, the only one of the twelve which does not commemorate some occasion in the life of Christ or the Virgin Mary, is observed each year on September 27th and is a strict fast day.

In memory of this Elevation of the Cross by Patriarch Macarius, the following prayer was composed: "Thy Cross do we adore, O Master, and Thy Holy Resurrection do we glorify."

TROPARION

O Lord, save Thy people and bless Thine inheritance, granting victories to the Orthodox Christians over their enemies and by Thy Cross upholding Thy community.

KONDAKION

Do Thou, Who wast of Thine own will lifted upon the Cross, grant Thy bounties upon the new state, O Christ our God; lift up in Thy power the Orthodox Christians, granting them victories over their adversaries; having Thy assistance the armament of peace, and invisible victory.

As the worshipers bow down to the Cross decorated with flowers on this feast day, the following prayer is sung three times: Thy Cross we adore and bow down in worship, Master Lord, and Thy Holy Resurrection we glorify.

St. Helena and Macarius

95

PRESENTATION TO THE TEMPLE OF THE VIRGIN MARY

Joachim and his wife, Anna, descendants of King David, had prayed that they might have a child and made a solemn promise that if a child were born to them it would be dedicated to the service of God. A daughter, Mary, was born to them and they did not forget their promise.

When Mary was three years old, Joachim and Anna assembled all of their relatives and friends and in a grand procession accompanied by lighted candles and the singing of holy songs, they led their daughter to the Temple in Jerusalem.

Many young virgins and aged widows lived in the Temple; having consecrated their lives to the service of the Lord. They studied the Word of God and then taught others. They also cleaned and decorated the Temple. The remainder of their time was spent in prayer.

Three-year-old Mary, without any assistance from her parents, climbed the huge stone steps leading to the entrance of the Temple where the High Priest awaited her.

The Priest led Mary not only into the Temple but also into the Holy of Holies, the Sanctuary where only he had the right to enter and then only once a year. The High Priest did this because he had been endowed with the power to see into the future just as other Bible prophets before him had foreseen events of the future. The Priest knew that Mary was to become the mother of the Saviour.

Mary remained in the Temple until she was fourteen years old. She spent most of her time studying with the priests, learning the Word of God. The rest of the time she spent in prayer.

Under the religious customs followed in the Old Testament, a virgin of the Temple was betrothed to some good man when she reached a certain age. This man would give her the protection of a husband without her becoming his wife. Mary was thus betrothed to one of her kinsman, a devout man named Joseph who lived in the town of Nazareth and worked as a carpenter.

Mary went to Nazareth to live with Joseph. She busied herself with the household chores but also found time to read many religious books and to commune often with God through prayer.

Mary's entrance into the Temple, the Presentation to the Temple of the Virgin Mary is one of the important feast days of the Eastern Orthodox Church. It is commemorated each year on December 4th.

TROPARION
Today is the prefiguration of the beneficence of God, and the heralding of the salvation of man: the Virgin brightly appears in the temple of God, and predicts Christ to all. Unto her let us also cry out aloud: Hail, thou who art the fulfillment of the Creator's providence.

KONDAKION
The most-pure temple of the Saviour, the most precious bridal-chamber and Virgin, the sacred treasury of the glory of God, today is led into the house of the Lord, she that bringeth the grace which is in the Divine Spirit; Whom the angels of God hymn: This is She Who is the Heavenly Abode.

NATIVITY OF THE SAVIOUR

The Christmas story, as it is beautifully told in the gospels of St. Matthew and St. Luke, is well known. The birth of Christ is commemorated as one of the most joyful feast days of the Eastern Orthodox Church. In importance, it is surpassed only by Easter.

During the reign of the Emperor Augustus as head of the Roman Empire, a decree was issued that a census was to be taken. In the Holy Land, every Israelite was instructed to go to the town of his family's origin for the census count. Judea's ruler at the time was King Herod, a wicked man who was feared and disliked by the people.

Joseph and Mary, both of them descendants of King David, were to go to Bethlehem, called the City of David, to be enrolled in the census. Bethlehem was a small town and when Joseph and Mary arrived they could find no place for lodging.

Night was falling and as there was no room for them at the inn, Joseph and Mary took refuge in a lowly stable, a cave-like place used by shepherds in herding their flocks when the weather was stormy. Here, at midnight, Mary gave birth to a son, Jesus. Wrapping the Infant in swaddling clothes she laid Him upon the straw in the manger. The prophecy of Micah was thus fulfilled and in this lowly manner began the Greatest Life Ever Lived.

As shepherds watched their flocks in the clear, beautiful night, a great brightness came about, turning the dusk into daylight. The shepherds were afraid.

An angel appeared and calmed them, saying, "Fear not, for I bring you tidings of great joy, which shall come to all people. Today in Bethlehem, the City of David, the Saviour Jesus who is Christ the Lord is born. This shall be a sign to you and you shall find the Infant lying in a manger and wrapped in swaddling clothes."

A multitude of angels then appeared, glorifying God and singing, "Glory to God in the highest, and on earth peace, good will toward men." After the angels had disappeared, the great light faded and the darkness of the night settled down over the land.

The shepherds decided to go to Bethlehem to see this Wonder that was heralded by the angels. These men who tended flocks hastened to the city where they found Mary and Joseph and the Infant Jesus who was lying in a manger.

After falling to their knees to adore Him, the shepherds told of the appearance of the angels and of the radiance in the skies and the celestial hosts singing together. Mary, the Mother of God, listened to their story and kept the words of the angel in her heart.

Christmas eve marks the beginning of twelve days of celebration in the Eastern Orthodox Church. As the first star appears on the eve of Christmas, Orthodox families break a day-long fast and hold a family holy supper. Midnight matin services in church follow.

In observance of Christmas, carolers in traditional native costumes visit the homes of members of the Church, singing Yule-tide songs and enacting religious skits. The Nativity of Jesus is observed on January 7th among the Eastern Orthodox Churches following the old Julian calendar with some Orthodox Churches, such as the Greek, celebrating the date on December 25th, as set by the Gregorian calendar used by most countries of the world.

THE HOLY SUPPER

The Holy Supper is a traditional family meal that is partaken of on Christmas Eve. First of all, straw is spread on the table and covered with a white tablecloth. A sheaf of straw is also left under an icon in the room. The straw serves as a reminder that the Christ Child was born in a lowly manger.

A single candle is placed in the center of the table and is lighted to represent the Star of Bethlehem and also as a symbol of Christ as the Light of the world.

In times past, the master of the house prepared a meal for all of the animals of the household and they were fed first. At the start of the family meal, the master of the home asked, "Have the animals been fed?" and after an affirmative reply the meal proceeded. This is a reminder that there were animals present at the time of the birth of Christ.

The meal traditionally consists of twelve Lenten dishes—twelve to symbolize the twelve original Apostles chosen by Christ to preach His gospel.

The head of the household begins the meal by breaking a roll and giving everyone at the table a portion of it. This symbolizes Christ at the Last Supper. After the meal the family goes to church in a body.

TROPARION

Thy nativity, O Christ our God, hath shown forth upon the world the light of Wisdom: for at it those that worshiped the stars were taught by a star to adore Thee, the Sun of Righteousness, and to know Thee, the Orient from on high. O Lord, glory to Thee.

KONDAKION

The Virgin today brings forth the Omnipotent, and the earth offers a cave to the Unapproachable. Angels give glory with shepherds, and the Magi journey with the star, and for our sake was born as a young child, He Who is God before all ages.

EPIPHANY—BAPTISM OF CHRIST

When Jesus was thirty years old, He came to the river Jordan to be baptized by John. Called the Forerunner, John the Baptist was the last of a long line of prophets who foretold of the coming of the Messiah.

Repeating the words of the angel concerning his son at the time of his birth, Zachary, the father of John the Baptist, had said, "He shall be the forerunner of the Saviour and shall prepare the way for Him."

John the Forerunner went into the wilderness when he was still quite young. He lived alone and clothed himself in the type of garment worn by prophets who lived long before his time—a robe of camel skin. His food consisted only of honey, locusts and wild roots. John spent his time doing penance, praying, and preparing himself for God's calling.

When John came out of the wilderness to preach on the banks of the river Jordan, he said, "Repent, for the Kingdom of Heaven is at hand. Prepare yourselves to accept the Saviour. He comes after me. As a sign of your repentance, come and be baptized. I baptize you with water, but He shall baptize you with the Holy Spirit."

Great numbers repented their sins and were baptized by John in the river Jordan. Many travelers passed the place where John preached and people soon began to call this prophet of the wilderness John the Baptist. Because of John's righteous living, many believed that he was the promised Messiah but he told them that Jesus was already on earth among the people but as yet none of them knew Him.

When Jesus came to be baptized, John recognized Him as the Messiah and said, "I should be baptized by You, and do You come to me?" Jesus replied that it should be done in order to fulfill all righteousness.

When Jesus stepped into the waters of the Jordan to be baptized, the heavens suddenly opened and the Holy Spirit descended in the form of a dove and rested on Him. The voice of God came down from heaven, saying, "This is My beloved Son in Whom I am well pleased."

The baptism of Jesus in the river Jordan by John the Baptist serves to explain the Holy Trinity—Father, Son and Holy Spirit. God the Father, spoke from Heaven, Christ, the Son of God, was baptized, and the Holy Spirit descended in the form of a dove.

The Baptism of Christ, one of the twelve important feast days, is observed each year on January 19th. This day is known as the Manifestation of the Most Holy Trinity and also as Epiphany or Theophany.

TROPARION

When in the Jordan Thou was baptized, O Lord, the worship of the Trinity was made manifest: for the voice of the Parent bear witness unto Thee, calling Thee His beloved Son, and the Spirit, in the vision of a dove, confirmed the certainty of the word. Thou that hast appeared, O Christ our God, and dost enlighten the world, glory to Thee.

KONDAKION

Thou hast appeared today to the universe, and Thy Light, O Lord, hath showed a sign upon us, who in knowledge sing unto Thee: Thou hast come, and hast appeared, O Light Unapproachable.

MEETING OF THE LORD IN THE TEMPLE

According to the religious custom followed by the Jewish people, every Israelite mother brought her first-born son to the Temple forty days after the birth of the child and offered him to God. This religious observance was in remembrance of the flight of the Children of Israel from Egypt and their escape from slavery.

In observation of the established custom, Mary and Joseph, the parents of Jesus, took Him to Jerusalem, which was not far from their home in Bethlehem, and brought Jesus to the Temple. There, as prescribed by the Jewish religious laws, Mary offered the Infant Christ Child to God.

Under the Jewish religious tenets, if a child's parents were wealthy, a lamb and a young pigeon or a turtle dove were offered as a sacrifice in the Temple. If the child's parents were poor, they offered two pigeons or two turtle doves. Joseph and Mary had little earthly wealth so they offered two turtle doves.

At the entrance to the Temple, Joseph and Mary met an aged holy man of Jerusalem named Simeon. The coming of the Messiah was awaited by Simeon because he had been promised by the Holy Spirit that he would not die until he had seen the Saviour of the world with his own eyes.

The Holy Spirit making this promise to Simeon had led the venerable holy man to the Temple on this day and when Simeon saw the Infant he knew at once that the Child was the promised Messiah.

Earlier in life, Simeon was one of the translators of the Old Testament. He had been assigned the task of translating the Book of Isaiah and when he came to the verse where Isaiah foretold that Jesus would be born of a Virgin, Simeon was puzzled and wanted to erase the word "virgin" and substitute the word "woman."

At this moment an angel appeared to him and commanded him to write the word "virgin," and was promised that before he would die he would see the fulfillment of this prophecy.

When Simeon saw Mary and the Child, he took Jesus in his arms and in thankfulness to God said a prayer which has become known as St. Simeon's Prayer and which is now sung at every Vesper service in Eastern Orthodox Churches.

After finishing his prayer, Simeon turned to Mary and told her that because of her Son there would be many arguments among the people. Some would be saved through Him but others would refuse to accept His teachings. Simeon also told Mary that her own heart would be pierced by a sword, meaning that she would undergo great suffering.

Living in the Temple at the time was an 84-year-old widow named Anna who spent her time fasting and praying as she also awaited the coming of the Saviour. When she saw the Infant Jesus, Anna praised God just as Simeon had done.

This feast day is observed each year on February 15 and it is customary to bless candles for use in homes on this day.

In remembrance of the bringing of the Infant Jesus to the Temple by Joseph and Mary, children of the Eastern Orthodox faith are also brought to the Church on the fortieth day after their birth. This is called incorporation with the Church.

TROPARION

Hail, O Virgin, birth-giver of God, full of grace; for from thee hath shone forth the Sun of Righteousness, Christ our God, Who giveth light to those who are in the darkness. Rejoice also, thou aged, righteous man, who didst receive in thine arms the Redeemer of our souls, Who bestoweth upon us the resurrection.

KONDAKION

Thou, who by Thy birth didst sanctify the Virgin's womb and didst bless the arms of Simeon, as was met, didst preserve and now hast saved us, O Christ our God. But give peace amid the alarm of wars to Thy community, and establish the Church, which Thou hast adopted into Thy love, O Thou Who alone lovest mankind.

ANNUNCIATION OF THE MOTHER OF GOD

Six months after an angel had appeared to Zachary in the Temple and had told him that his wife Elizabeth would bear him a son who was to become John the Baptist, the Archangel Gabriel appeared to the Virgin Mary.

She was deep in prayer and the Archangel said to her, "Rejoice! Mary, full of grace; the Lord is with you: blessed are you among women."

Mary was startled when she heard these words and her mind was troubled. She wondered what the angel's greeting meant. Seeing her distress, Gabriel hastened to relieve her anxiety by telling her further:

"Fear not, Mary, you have found favor with God. You shall give birth to a Son. You shall name Him Jesus. He shall be great and shall be called the Son of the Most High. He shall be given the throne of David and shall rule over Israel and there shall be no end to His kingdom."

Mary then asked, "How shall this happen to me?"

In reply, the Archangel said that the Holy Spirit would descend upon her and the power of God would overshadow her. The Child would be called the Son of God. To confirm his words, the Archangel Gabriel then told Mary that Elizabeth, who was her counsin, would also have a son.

Mary believed the angel and said, "Behold, the servant of the Lord; let it be unto me according to your word." The angel then departed.

Having learned from the angel that her cousin, Elizabeth, was to give birth to a son, the Blessed Virgin visited her. When she saw Mary, Elizabeth, who was to be the mother of John the Baptist, exclaimed, "Blessed are you among women, and blessed is the fruit of your womb! Whom am I that the mother of my Lord should come to me?" Mary then began to pray.

Elizabeth, in this conversation, was the first to call the Virgin Mary the Mother of God. Mary stayed with her cousin Elizabeth for three months and then returned to her own home.

The message of the Archangel Gabriel to the Virgin Mary is commemorated in the Eastern Orthodox Church as the Feast of the Annunciation and is observed each year on April 7th. The visit of the Archangel Gabriel to the Virgin Mary is portrayed on the icon in the center of the Royal Doors of the Iconostas.

TROPARION

Today is the beginning of our salvation and the manifestation of the mystery which is from eternity: the Son of God becometh the Son of a Virgin, and Gabriel announceth the glad tidings of grace. Wherefore, let us also cry out with him unto the Mother of God: Hail, Thou that art full of grace, the Lord is with Thee.

KONDAKION

O Queen of the Heavenly Host, Defender of our souls! In that we are delivered from evil, as thy servants, O Mother of God, we offer unto Thee the songs of thanks and victory. But inasmuch as thou hast power invincible, from all calamity deliver us, that we may cry unto thee: Hail, O Ever-Virgin Bride!

PALM SUNDAY—ENTRY OF THE LORD INTO JERUSALEM

The Feast of the Passover, observed by Jewish people who follow the Old Testament, coincides with the Easter season of the Eastern Orthodox Church. As the Jewish Passover approached and Jesus was nearing the end of His time on earth, many people gathered in Jerusalem to pray in the Temple.

Following the performance of the miracle when He raised Lazarus from the dead, Christ and His disciples were among those making the journey to Jerusalem to observe the Feast of the Passover.

Approaching Jerusalem, Jesus and His followers stopped just outside the city at the Mount of Olives. The Master selected two of the disciples and sent them to the nearby town of Bethphage. "Go into the village," He told them, "and as soon as you enter it you will find a colt tied upon which no man has ever sat. Loosen him and bring the colt to Me."

The disciples did as Jesus instructed them and brought the colt. Then, after the disciples had spread their garments on the colt, Jesus sat thereon and rode into Jerusalem.

The crowds along the road, making their way toward the city for their pilgrimage to Jerusalem, saw Jesus riding on the colt with His disciples surrounding Him and they greeted Him with great joy. Most of them knew of the great miracle Christ had performed in raising Lazarus from the dead.

Although Christ knew that in this entrance He was going to His trial, final suffering, crucifixion and death, the multitudes believed that Jesus was riding into Jerusalem to become the earthly King of Israel. They shouted loudly, "Hosanna, to the Son of David. Blessed is He that cometh in the name of the Lord. Hosanna in the highest."

The great crowds along the way spread their garments before Christ. Some of them cut branches from the trees and strewed them in the path before Him. Others carried the branches.

There were many Pharisees and Scribes (leaders in Jewish religion) among the crowd and when they heard the joyous shouting of the people and observed the homage paid to Jesus, they asked Christ to rebuke His disciples for being so noisy. Jesus answered them, "I tell you that if they should hold their peace, the stones would cry out."

After arriving in Jerusalem, Jesus went to the Temple where He began to cast out those who bought and sold in the House of Worship. He overthrew the tables of the money changers and toppled the seats of those who sold doves for use in sacrifice. He said, "It is written, My home shall be called the house of prayer but you have made it a den of thieves."

The crowds that followed Jesus increased in size as new arrivals swelled the ranks. The sick, the lame and the blind were brought to Jesus in the Temple and He cured them all. Even the children who were present cried out, "Hosanna to the Son of David."

The Pharisees, seeing all these wonderful works performed by Jesus, became more and more enraged.

The entrance of Jesus into Jerusalem had been long before foretold by the prophet Zachariah. The prophet had said, "Rejoice greatly, daughter of Zion, and shout, O daughter of Jerusalem; behold thy King cometh to thee. He is just, and having salvation; lowly, and riding upon a colt."

On this Sunday, observed the week before Easter, green branches are blessed in Eastern Orthodox churches. Palm branches were used for Christ's triumphal entry into Jerusalem and from this has come the name, Palm Sunday. In America, where Easter usually comes early in the spring before the buds have opened in their first greenery, branches of the pussy willow are used.

In Eastern Orthodox churches, blessed willow branches are given to the worshipers who hold them in their hands during the Liturgy. Sometimes lighted candles are also held. The blessed willow branches are taken home by parishioners and draped above the frames of icons and religious pictures.

TROPARION
O Christ our God, Thou didst raise Lazarus from the dead, and thus before Thy Passion didst declare certain the general Resurrection. Wherefore we also, like the children, carry emblems of victory and greet Thee, O Conqueror of Death, with the cry: Hosanna in the Highest! Blessed is He that cometh in the name of the Lord.

KONDAKION
On a throne in heaven, borne on a foal upon the earth, Thou didst, O Christ our God, accept the praise of the angels, and the hymn of the children that cried unto Thee: Blessed art Thou that comest to recall Adam.

LESSER FEAST DAYS

(All dates new calendar)

Feast of St. Basil the Great. (New Year's Day)	January 14
Feast of the Three Saints: Basil the Great Gregory the Theologian St. John of Chrysostom	February 12
St. George, Great Martyr and Victory-Bearer	May 6
Feast of Saints Cyril and Methodius	May 24
Nativity of John the Baptist	July 7
Feast of Saints Peter and Paul	July 12
Feast of St. Vladimir	July 28
Day of the Prophet Elijah	August 2
Beheading of John the Baptist (A day of fasting)	September 11
Protection of the Virgin Mary	October 14
Great Martyr Demetrius, the Wonderworker	November 8
Feast of St. Michael the Archangel and Other Angels	November 21
Feast of St. Nicholas	December 19

6

Brief

Orthodox

Catechism

AN ORTHODOX CATECHISM
I. INTRODUCTION

What is a Catechism?
A Catechism is a short exposition of the doctrines of the Lord Jesus Christ in question and answer form.

Why are the teachings of Christ necessary for us?
To lead us to God, to salvation and to happiness.

How do we come near to God?
By thought, wish and deed. By thought in believing in Him; by wish in praying to Him and by deed in fulfilling the will and Law of God.

From what source may we learn how to believe in God?
The Creed.

From what source do we learn to pray?
The Lord's Prayer.

From what source do we learn to live according to the will and Law of God?
The Ten Commandments.

Where do we find Christ's teachings about happiness?
In the Beatitudes.

Why are we called Eastern Orthodox Christians?
We are Christians through believing in our Lord Jesus Christ and Eastern Orthodox Christians through believing in the teachings of the Eastern Orthodox Church.

II. THE CREED

What is the Creed?
It is a short expounding of the Orthodox faith, composed at the first two Ecumenical Councils, and consisting of twelve articles.

What is an Ecumenical Council?
An assembly of the clergy from all parts of the world.

THE FIRST ARTICLE

How does the first article of the Creed read?
I believe in One God, the Father Almighty, Maker of heaven and earth, and of all things visible and invisible.

Who is spoken of in the first article?
God the Father.

What is meant by the words, "I believe"?
A belief that all the teachings of the Faith in this Creed are true.

Who is God?
God is a spirit, eternal, all-good, omniscient, all-just, almighty, omnipresent, all-sufficing, never-changing and all-blessed. From Him everything originated and by Him everything is sustained.

What is revealed to us concerning the Holy Trinity?
God is One but is Trine in Person—God the Father, God the Son, and God the Holy Spirit—an Undivided and Consubstantial Trinity.

What difference is there between the Persons of the Holy Trinity?
God the Father is neither begotten nor proceeds from any other person. The Son of God is from all eternity begotten of the Father; the Holy Spirit, from all eternity, proceeds from the Father. The three Persons of the Holy Trinity are of equal Divine majesty.

Why is God called Almighty?
He upholds all things in His power and His will.

Why is God called the Maker?
He created the heaven and the earth, and all things visible and invisible.

What is meant by the word "invisible"?
The unseen spiritual world which includes incorporeal Angels who have intelligence, will and power.

What is meant by the word "Angel"?
A messenger, because God sends the Angels to announce His will to the people. There are also evil Angels who do not obey God and teach evil to the people.

What is a Guardian Angel?
An Angel given to us from God at the time of our baptism to guard us from evil.

What do we know of the visible world?
In the beginning, God created the visible world in six days and, lastly, and in His image, man.

Does God take care of the world?
Yes, He preserves and directs it.

THE SECOND ARTICLE

How does the second article of the Creed read?
And in one Lord Jesus Christ, the only begotten Son of God, begotten of the Father before all ages. Light of Light, True God of True God, begotten, not created, being of one substance with the Father, through Whom all things were made.

Who is spoken of in the second article?
Jesus Christ, the Son of God; the Second Person of the Holy Trinity.

What does the name Jesus Christ mean?
Jesus means Savior and Christ means Anointed.

Why is Christ called the Son of God, the Only Begotten?
He is the only Son of God, begotten of the substance of God the Father. Begotten before all ages, He is eternal.

What is meant by the words, "Light of Light, True God of True God"?
God the Father and God the Son are one indivisible Divine person just as light appears simultaneously with the rising of the sun. Just as the Father is True God, so also the Son is True God.

Why is it said, "begotten, not created"?
This is stated to contradict the false doctrine of Arius, who taught that Jesus Christ was mortal and not of Divine creation.

What is meant by "of one substance with the Father"?
Jesus Christ is of one and the same substance with God the Father and has the same Divine nature as God.

What is meant by the words "through Whom all things were made"?
God the Father created all things through His Son.

THE THIRD ARTICLE

How does the third article of the Creed read?
Who for us men, and for our salvation, came down from heaven and was incarnate of the Holy Spirit and the Virgin Mary and became Man.

What is spoken of in this article?
The Son of God came from heaven to save the people from sin, the curse, and death. God has always been both in heaven and on earth. Invisible before, He afterwards became a visible mortal, taking upon himself the flesh and soul of man.

What is meant by the words "and was incarnate"?
The Son of God took upon Himself human form, except sin, without ceasing to be God. He was incarnated from the Holy Spirit and the Virgin Mary.

Who was the Virgin Mary?
The Blessed Virgin Mary was of the family of Abraham and David, the lineage of Israel that was given the promise of the Savior. She is called the Ever-Virgin because she always was and is a virgin.

How does the Eastern Orthodox Church teach of the dignity of the Virgin Mary?
The Orthodox Church gives her the title of "Mother of God" (Theotokos) and honors her far above the cherubim and seraphim.

THE FOURTH ARTICLE

How does the fourth article of the Creed read?
And was crucified for us under Pontius Pilate, and suffered, and was buried.

What is spoken of in this article?
The suffering and death of Jesus Christ.

Being God, how could Christ suffer?
He suffered and died as man, by His own good will, for our sins. He actually suffered all the pain and torture of a death on the cross.

What does the reference to Pontius Pilate express?
Pontius Pilate was the Roman governor of Judea. He conducted the trial of Jesus. The reference to Pilate indicates the time of the crucifixion.

THE FIFTH ARTICLE

How does the fifth article of the Creed read?
And rose again the third day according to the Scriptures.

What is spoken of in this article?
The Resurrection of Jesus Christ on the third day after His death.

By what power did Christ rise from the dead?
The power of His Divinity.

How does the Resurrection of Christ affect us?
Christ, having risen from the grave, obtained victory over death and made possible to all believers Resurrection and life eternal.

What is meant by the words "according to the Scriptures"?
Christ was born, lived on earth, suffered and died, and arose from the dead as had been foretold by prophets long before.

Did Christ appear on earth after His Resurrection?
Yes, ten times. His last appearance was forty days after the Resurrection.

THE SIXTH ARTICLE

How does the sixth article of the Creed read?
And ascended into heaven and sitteth at the right hand of the Father.

What is spoken of in this article?
The ascension of Jesus Christ into heaven.

When and how did Christ ascend into heaven?
His ascension, witnessed by all of His faithful disciples, took place on the Mount of Olives forty days after His Resurrection. His ascension was with His real human body.

What is signified by Christ's sitting beside His Father?
Christ has one and the same power, honor and glory together with God the Father.

THE SEVENTH ARTICLE

How does the seventh article of the Creed read?
And He shall come again with glory to judge the living and the dead. And His kingdom shall have no end.

What is spoken of in this article?
Christ will come again in glory, from heaven to earth, to judge all living people and those resurrected from the dead.

Who and what will Christ judge on His second coming?
The judgment will be the same for all people. Sinful deeds, words and thoughts will be condemned by the Lord.

When will Christ's second coming take place?
The time is not known, even to angels, but many signs of His second coming have been revealed to us. Love among the peoples of the earth will cease. Faith will decrease and sins will multiply. Calamities such as wars, pestilence and earthquakes will prevail and the antichrist will appear.

Who is antichrist?
The antichrist is the adversary of Jesus Christ who, by the power of Satan, will perform false miracles and strive to destroy Christianity. He will claim for himself the worship due to God but in the end the Lord will destroy him.

What is meant by "And His kingdom shall have no end"?
Christ will reign eternally over the righteous.

THE EIGHTH ARTICLE

How does the eighth article of the Creed read?
And I believe in the Holy Spirit, the Lord, the Giver of Life, Who proceedeth from the Father, who together with the Father and Son is worshiped and glorified. Who spake by the prophets.

Who is spoken of in this article?

The Holy Spirit, the third person of the Holy Trinity.

Why is the Holy Spirit called the "Giver of Life"?

Together with the Father and Son, He gives life to all creatures, especially spiritual life to men.

What is meant by the words, "Who proceedeth from the Father"?

The meaning is that the Holy Spirit does proceed from God the Father. Christ Himself said: ". . . the Spirit of truth, Who proceeded from the Father, He shall testify of Me."

What is meant by the words "Who together with the Father and Son is worshiped and glorified"?

The Holy Spirit equal with the Father and the Son while being together with them, and should be worshiped and glorified just as God the Father and God the Son are. This is indicated in Christ's command to baptize in the Name of the Father, and of the Son and of the Holy Spirit.

What is meant by the words "Who spake by the prophets"?

In the Old Testament the Holy Spirit spoke through the prophets just as He spoke through the Apostles in the New Testament. The books of the prophets as well as the writings of the Apostles were written under the inspiration of the Holy Spirit. The Holy Spirit is communicated to Christians through prayer and the Sacraments.

THE NINTH ARTICLE

How does the ninth article of the Creed read?

And in one Holy, Catholic and Apostolic Church.

What is spoken of in this article?

The Church.

What is the Church?

The Church is a body of Christians, united by the Seven Sacraments, the Hierarchy and the Orthodox faith.

Why is the Church one?

The Church is one because it has one Head, Christ, and but one Orthodox doctrine. The Church is the Body of Christ—He is to the Church what the soul is to the body.

Why is the Church holy?

It is sanctified by the doctrines and Passions of Christ.

Why is the Church Catholic?

Catholic means universal and the Church is universal because it includes all of the Orthodox believers of all lands, of all times and of all peoples.

Why is the Church Apostolic?

The Church is Apostolic because it was spread throughout the world by the Apostles and their successors, the bishops and priests.

What is the highest earthly authority of the Church?

The authority of the Ecumenical Council.

What is the highest authority in the provincial churches?

The Patriarch or Archbishop and his synod.

THE TENTH ARTICLE

How does the tenth article of the Creed read?

I acknowledge one Baptism for the remission of sins.

What is spoken of in this article?

The Sacrament of Baptism.

What is a Sacrament?
A Sacrament is a holy act through which the Grace of the Holy Spirit is given. It is a visible sign of invisible Divine Grace.

How many Sacraments are there?
Seven. They include Baptism, Chrismation, Communion, Penance, Ordination (the Priesthood), Matrimony and Unction with Oil.

What does Baptism consist of?
The believer, through being immersed three times in water in the name of the Father, and of the Son, and of the Holy Spirit, is born into spiritual life.

What does Chrismation consist of?
The baptized believer is anointed with Holy Chrism (Holy Oil blessed by Bishops) as the seal of the gift of the Holy Spirit.

What does the Sacrament of Communion consist of?
In the form of bread and wine, believers partake of the very Body and Blood of Christ.

When was the Sacrament of Communion instituted?
At the Last Supper by Jesus when He blessed bread, broke it and gave it to the disciples and took the chalice and gave thanks and gave it to them to drink.

How do Orthodox Christians receive Communion?
In the form of bread and wine—the very Body and Blood of Christ.

What does Penance consist of?
Confession of sins by the believer before a priest with forgiveness from God then received.

What does the Sacrament of Ordination (Holy Orders) consist of?
The ordained, by the laying on of hands of the Bishops, receive the grace to minister the Sacraments.

How many degrees of Priesthood are there?
Three. Bishops, Priests and Deacons.

How do these differ?
Deacons serve at the Sacraments; Priests perform the Sacraments with the exception of Ordination; and Bishops perform all of the Sacraments.

What does the Sacrament of Matrimony consist of?
The union of man and woman in wedlock is blessed in the image of the union of Christ with His church.

What does Unction with Oil consist of?
The sick, anointed with oil, receive from God the grace of becoming healed.

THE ELEVENTH ARTICLE

How does the eleventh article of the Creed read?
I look for the Resurrection of the dead.

What is spoken of in this article?
All of the dead will arise again at the end of the world and become immortal.

What shall become of the people living at the time of the second coming of Christ?
Their bodies shall be changed and they, also, shall become immortal.

THE TWELFTH ARTICLE

How does the twelfth article of the Creed read?
And the life in the world to come. Amen.

What is spoken of in this article?
After the general Resurrection there shall be, to the just, an eternal life of blessedness, and for the unrepentant sinners, an everlasting life of torment.

III. THE LORD'S PRAYER

Why is this prayer called the Lord's Prayer?

It was given to the Apostles and to all Christians by the Lord Jesus Christ Himself.

How is the Lord's Prayer divided?

Into the Invocation, the Seven Petitions and the Doxology.

How does the Invocation read?

Our Father, Who art in Heaven. We call God our Father because we love Him, as children love their father.

How does the first petition read?

Hallowed be Thy Name.

What do we ask of God in this petition?

We ask God to help us keep His Holy Name in our minds and hearts and that we may live according to His law and thus glorify Him among people.

How does the second petition read?

Thy Kingdom come.

What do we ask of God in this petition?

We ask His help that the Spirit of God may lead us to good and to happiness and that sin should not reign in us.

How does the third petition read?

Thy will be done on earth as it is in Heaven.

What do we ask of God in this petition?

We ask that all things in our life should come through the Will of God.

How does the fourth petition read?

Give us this day our daily bread.

What do we ask of God in this petition?

We ask God to provide all of our daily needs for the present day—food, clothing and shelter.

How does the fifth petition read?

And forgive us our trespasses, as we forgive those who trespass against us.

What do we ask of God in this petition?

We ask that God forgive our sins as we, in turn, forgive those who have done wrongs to us. If we do not forgive others, God will not forgive us.

How does the sixth petition read?

And lead us not into temptation.

What do we ask of God in this petition?

We ask God to drive away the temptations that lead us to sin. These temptations come from ourselves, from evil people, and from Satan.

How does the seventh petition read?

But deliver us from evil.

What do we ask of God in this petition?

We ask God to keep us and protect us from evil and misfortune.

How does the doxology of the Lord's Prayer read?

For Thine is the Kingdom, and the Power, and the Glory forever and ever. Amen.

What does this doxology express?

Through it we express the hope that God will grant us all our petitions because everything is within His Power and Might.

IV. THE TEN COMMANDMENTS

Who gave the Ten Commandments?

The Lord God Himself, through the prophet Moses, gave the Commandments on Mount Sinai on the fiftieth day of the Exodus of the Hebrews from Egypt.

Why must Christians keep the Ten Commandments?

Christ Himself instructed Christians to keep the Commandments as recorded in the Gospel.

What is the first commandment?

I am the Lord thy God; thou shalt have no other gods before Me.

What are we commanded to do by this commandment?

We must acknowledge God in thought; believe in Him with our heart, and love Him; to glorify Him by words of our mouth, and to serve Him with our whole being.

What regard should we have for the Angels and for the Saints of God?

We should venerate them as the servants of God; because of their love for us they pray to God for us.

What are the sins against the first commandment?

Serving other false gods instead of the One True God, failing to pray to God in the home and non-attendance at church.

What is the second commandment?

Thou shalt not make unto thee any graven image or any likeness of anything that is in heaven above, or that is in the earth beneath, or that is in the water under the earth. Thou shalt not worship them, nor serve them.

What does God forbid in this commandment?

The worship of idols.

What is an idol?

An idol is a hand-wrought statue or figure serving as a representation of a false deity, such as the golden calf fashioned by the Hebrews and worshiped as their god.

What is an Icon?

Icons are the Holy Pictures used in Eastern Orthodox churches to represent Jesus Christ, the Virgin Mary and the Saints. They are correctly used for religious remembrance, and prayers to God and the Saints are offered before them because in so doing we raise our minds and hearts to God and the Saints portrayed on the Icons.

What is the third commandment?

Thou shalt not take the name of the Lord thy God in vain.

What is forbidden by this commandment?

The use of the name of God in a wrong way.

When may the name of God be used?

In prayers, in the instruction of religion and when lawful authority requires the swearing of an oath.

What is the fourth commandment?

Remember the Sabbath day to keep it holy. Six days shalt thou labor and do all thy work; but the seventh day is the Sabbath of the Lord thy God.

What does this commandment require of us?

Six days are for work but the seventh day is dedicated to God for church attendance, for visiting the sick and for other good deeds.

Why does God command us to keep the seventh day holy?
God created the world in six days and on the seventh day He rested. The word Sabbath is from the Hebrew and means day of rest. In Old Testament times Saturday was the seventh day and was observed as the Sabbath but Christians consecrate Sunday, the first day of the week to commemorate the Resurrection of Christ.

What other Orthodox days beside Sunday should we consecrate?
The holy days honoring the Lord, the Virgin Mary and the Saints. Fasting days should also be observed.

What is the fifth commandment?
Honor thy father and thy mother, that thy days may be long upon the land which the Lord thy God giveth thee.

What does God require of us in this commandment?
He commands us to honor, respect and obey our parents. We are also expected to respect those who stand in place of parents such as the government, spiritual fathers and teachers.

What is the sixth commandment?
Thou shalt not kill.

What does God forbid in this commandment?
He forbids the taking of human life by force or guile and forbids strife, hatred and cruelty which may shorten life.

What is the seventh commandment?
Thou shalt not commit adultery.

What does God forbid in this commandment?
He forbids unclean thoughts, feelings, words and deeds and lustful pleasures. It is also sinful to read obscene books, to sing or listen to immoral songs or to look at shameless pictures and entertainment.

What is the eighth commandment?
Thou shalt not steal.

What does God forbid in this commandment?
He forbids the taking of things that belong to others, either by open force or secretly.

What is the ninth commandment?
Thou shalt not bear false witness against thy neighbor.

What does God forbid in this commandment?
He forbids us to testify falsely against any person in court or to slander or defame anyone.

What is the tenth commandment?
Thou shalt not covet thy neighbor's house, thou shalt not covet thy neighbor's wife, nor his manservant, nor his maidservant, nor his ox, nor his ass, nor anything that is thy neighbor's.

What does God forbid in this commandment?
He forbids us to do evil by covetous means. Evil desires may lead to evil deeds.

7

Prayers and Orthodoxy

PRAYERS

ORTHODOX COMMANDMENTS

ORTHODOX SACRAMENTS

WORKS OF MERCY — TRUTHS

RULES FOR CHRISTIAN LIVING

EXAMINATION OF CONSCIENCE

SYMBOLISM

BAPTISMAL NAMES

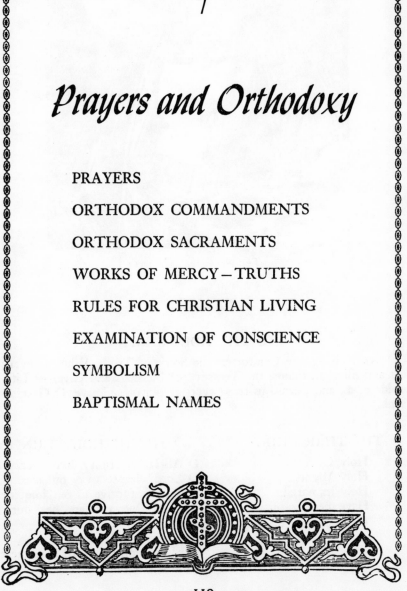

The Archangel Michael

PRAYERS

TO THE HOLY SPIRIT

O Heavenly King, the Comforter, the Spirit of Truth, Who art everywhere present and fillest all things; the Treasury of Blessings and Giver of Life, come and abide in us, and cleanse us from every impurity and save, O Gracious One, our souls.

THE THRICE-HOLY

Holy God,
Holy Mighty
Holy Immortal,
Have mercy on us.
(Repeated three times)

TO THE HOLY TRINITY

O All-Holy Trinity, have mercy on us.
O Lord, cleanse away our sins:
O Master, forgive us our iniquities;
O Holy One, visit and heal our
  infirmities,
For Thy name's sake.
Lord have mercy. Lord have mercy.
  Lord have mercy.

TO THE ALL-HOLY VIRGIN

Hail, O Mother of God and Virgin Mary, full of grace,
the Lord is with thee; blessed art thou among women
and blessed is the fruit of thy womb, for thou has
borne the Saviour of our souls.

TO THE GUARDIAN ANGEL

O Angel of God, my holy Guardian, given to me from heaven, protect and enlighten me this day, give me strength to overcome temptations and save me from all evil. Teach me to do what is right and guide me in the steps of Christ, my Saviour. AMEN

MORNING PRAYER

O God, cleanse me, a sinner, inasmuch as I have never done any good thing before Thee. Deliver me from all evil, and let Thy will abide within me, so that I may open my unworthy lips to praise Thy holy name of the Father, and of the Son, and of the Holy Spirit, now and always, and unto ages and ages. AMEN

EVENING PRAYER

O Lord our God, forgive me all the sins I have committed this day in word, deed and in thought. Grant unto me peaceful and undisturbed sleep, send Thy guardian angel to shelter and protect me, for Thou art the preserver of our souls and bodies, and to Thee we ascribe glory to the Father, and to the Son, and to the Holy Spirit, now and ever, unto ages and ages. AMEN

GRACE BEFORE MEALS

O Lord, bless the food and drink of Thy servants and make us mindful of the needs of others. AMEN

Bless us, O Lord, and these Thy gifts, which we are about to receive from Thy bounty, through Christ our Lord. AMEN

GRACE AFTER MEALS

We thank Thee, O Christ, our God, that Thou sated us with Thy goods of Thine earth; do not deprive us also of Thy heavenly kingdom. AMEN

We thank Thee, O Lord, that Thou hast satisfied us with Thy earthly gifts and we thank Thee for all Thy mercies and we bless Thy holy name always, now and ever and unto ages and ages.
AMEN

PRAYER OF SAINT MACARIUS THE GREAT

O God eternal and King of every creature who hast vouchsafed that I should live even down to the present hour, forgive me the sins which I have this day committed either in deed or word or in thought, and cleanse, O Lord, my humble soul from every defilement of body and spirit. And grant, O Lord, that I may, during this night, have a peaceful sleep so that on rising from my humble bed, I should continue to please Thy holy name through all the days of my life and obtain victory over the enemies—both bodily and incorporeal—that are assailing me. Deliver me, O Lord, also from frivolous thoughts that defile me, and from evil desires.

ST. EPHRAIM THE SYRIAN'S PRAYER OF PENANCE

O Lord and Master of my life, take from me the spirit of sloth, faint-heartedness, lust of power, and idle talk. But give rather the spirit of chastity, humility, patience and love to Thy servant. Yes, O Lord and King, grant me to see my own errors and not to judge my brother, for Thou are blessed from all ages to ages. AMEN

SAINT SIMEON'S PRAYER

Lord, now lettest Thou Thy servant depart in peace, according to Thy word: For mine eyes have seen Thy salvation, Which Thou hast prepared before the face of all people: A light to lighten the Gentiles, and the glory of Thy people Israel. (Luke 2:29-33)

THE SEVEN CORPORAL WORKS OF MERCY

1. To feed the hungry.
2. To give drink to the thirsty.
3. To clothe the naked.
4. To visit the sick.
5. To harbor the harborless.
6. To visit and ransom the captives.
7. To bury the dead.

THE SEVEN SPIRITUAL WORKS OF MERCY

1. To admonish sinners.
2. To give instruction to the ignorant.
3. To give counsel to the doubtful.
4. To comfort those who sorrow.
5. To bear wrongs patiently.
6. To forgive all injuries.
7. To offer prayers for the living and the dead.

THE COMMANDMENTS OF THE ORTHODOX CHURCH

1. To keep holy the sainted days—Sundays and Holy Days.
2. To attend church and hear the service on Sundays and Holy Days.
3. To observe fasting on appointed days.
4. To confess our sins and receive Blessed Eucharist, at least once a year, during the Great Lent.
5. Not to solemnize marriage at forbidden times.
6. To pray daily—especially at the beginning and the end of the day.

THE SEVEN SACRAMENTS

1. The Sacrament of Baptism
2. The Sacrament of Holy Chrismation (Confirmation)
3. The Sacrament of Holy Communion (Holy Eucharist)
4. The Sacrament of Penance (Confession)
5. The Sacrament of Holy Orders (Priesthood)
6. The Sacrament of Holy Matrimony (Marriage)
7. The Sacrament of Prayer Oil (Unction with Oil)

THE TRUTHS OF THE ORTHODOX FAITH

1. There is One God, manifest in three equal Persons: God the Father, God the Son, and God the Holy Spirit.
2. As a Judge, God is just. He rewards the just through the Kingdom of Heaven and punishes the wicked through eternal damnation.
3. God the Son became mortal man to save all mankind from eternal damnation.
4. The human soul is immortal.
5. The Grace of God is an absolute necessity for salvation.

SOME RULES FOR CHRISTIAN LIVING

Be diligent in your work and shun idleness.
Speak the truth at all times.
Know when to speak and when to remain silent.
Do not positively affirm or deny things you know nothing about.
Respect your elders—listen when they speak.
Be not proud or covetous.
Do not delay making amends to those you offend.
Be kind to others and they will be kind to you.
Observe neatness and cleanliness in your habits and dress.

EXAMINATION OF CONSCIENCE BEFORE CONFESSION

Before going to Confession the penitent should make a self-appraisal of personal shortcomings. For guidance, the following questions are suitable for self-examination of conscience.

Have you experienced doubts in your faith? Have you despaired of God's mercies and spoken against the Lord in time of adversity?

Have you attended church regularly? Have you prayed regularly, remembering others in your prayers? Have you kept the Sabbath holy and refrained from doing any unnecessary work on Sundays or Holy Days?

Have you observed Lent and kept the fasts of the Church? Have you attended dances or indulged in entertainments during Lent?

Have you put your belief into fortune tellers or consulted those who presume to predict the future?

Have you spoken lightly of religious matters or of sacred objects? Have you taken the name of God in vain? Have you cursed yourself or others?

Have you become angry at others or caused others to anger?

Have you honored your parents, superiors, teachers and spiritual advisors? Have you shown respect to the infirm and the aged?

Have you oppressed anyone, held hatred for others, envied others or desired revenge on anyone? Have you injured anyone by word or deed? Have you caused strife between others? Have you desired or hastened the death of anyone?

Have you chosen your companions wisely? Have you wilfully entertained impure thoughts or desires? Have you read obscene literature or been guilty of unchaste words or actions?

Have you taken any property belonging to others? Have you deceived anyone in business transactions? Have you coveted the possessions of others?

Have you witnessed falsely against anyone or passed unconfirmed judgment on anyone?

Have you partaken of confession and Holy Communion at least once a year?

CHURCH SYMBOLISM

Church symbolism dates back to the very beginnings of Christianity. During the persecution periods certain symbols were used to decorate the places of worship with these symbols having specified religious meanings. Few early Christians could read but all of them could recognize the symbolic portrayals. Many of these symbols are still used in church decorations and may be seen in the designs of stained glass windows, carved woodwork and icons.

Listed here are some of the most familiar Christian symbols.

ALPHA-OMEGA (AΩ)—The first and last letters of the Greek alphabet. Signifies that God is the beginning and end of all things. Also expresses the eternity and divinity of the Lord and is referred to in the Book of Revelation of the Bible.

ANCHOR—Symbol of a belief and hope in God.

BOOK—A symbol of the Gospel—the Word of God.

BREAD—Symbol of the Divine Eucharist.

BUTTERFLY—One of the finest symbols of resurrection and eternal life. First the crawling larva representing the low estate of man on earth; second, the chrysalis depicting man in the grave; and finally the bursting forth in a beautiful body of the butterfly, in symbol of the resurrection of man's soul to a new glorified life in heaven.

CANDLES—Symbol of the light of the Word of God.

CENSER—The warmth of prayer, symbolized by incense.

CHALICE—Symbol of the Holy Communion and the brotherhood of man.

CROSS—There are many forms. All of them symbolize the Crucifixion of Christ and the triumph of Christianity.

CROWN OF THORNS—Symbol of the suffering of Christ.

EAGLE—Symbolizes St. John, who, because of his lofty theological expressions, soared heavenward like the eagle. A two-headed eagle signifies the Byzantine Empire and its church.

EYE—Symbol of the omniscience and omnipresence of God.

FISH—Early Christians used the fish as a secret symbol in the catacombs to conceal and safeguard their faith. The Greek word meaning fish (IXΘΥΣ) symbolizes Christ the Saviour, the Holy Eucharist and Christians.

FISHERMAN—Symbol of Christ the Saviour as a Fisher of Men.

FLOWERS—Symbol of the pleasures and beauties of paradise.

FROG—Because of the transformation in its life cycle, the frog was deemed an emblem of the progressive steps of Christianity.

HARE—A symbol of the speed with which life passes.

IC XC—Symbolizes Jesus Christ.

$\dfrac{IC \mid XC}{NI \mid KA}$ —Symbol meaning that Jesus Christ is victorious over all.

LAMB—A beautiful symbol of Jesus. Originates from John the Baptist's annunciation, "Behold the Lamb of God." The Lamb is usually depicted crowned with a three-rayed nimbus denoting divinity and carrying a banner of victory.

LAUREL—The emblem of martyr's glory.

LILY—The emblem of radiant purity.

LION—Sometimes an emblem of Christ. Usually St. Mark is symbolized by the lion because his Gospel begins with the call to repentance by John the Baptist, a voice crying in the wilderness which is compared to the roar of a lion in the desert.

OLIVE—Signifies consecration.

OLIVE BRANCH—An emblem of happiness and peace, symbolizing an end of turmoil as first mentioned in the Bible when the dove sent out by Noah returned with an olive branch.

OLIVE TREE—The emblem of immortality.

OX (OR BULL)—Symbolizes good deeds. St. Luke is symbolized by the ox because his Gospel begins with an account of the sacrifice of Zacharias. Luke also describes the sacrificial death of Christ and the ox or bull was the ancient sacrifice animal.

PALM—The emblem of Christianity's victory.

PEACOCK—A symbol of immortality. The peacock was a very popular symbol in early Christian days, representing the soul glorified.

PIGEON (OR DOVE) — Symbol of the Holy Spirit. At the Baptism of Christ by John the Baptist, the Holy Spirit descended in the form of a dove.

SHEEP—Followers of Christ—Christian worshipers.

SHEPHERD—Christ the Good Shepherd. The well-known 23rd Psalm calls the Lord a Shepherd.

SNAKE—Signifies evil and Satan. The first temptation to Eve in the Garden of Eden came through the whispering of the serpent.

TRIANGLE—Symbolic of the Holy Trinity.

VESSEL (OR SHIP)—Symbolizes the Church of Christ.

VINE—The body of the Church of Christ.

VINEYARD—Symbolizes the Holy Communion and also symbolic of Christ from whom we receive life as the grape plant does from the vineyard.

VIOLET—Symbol of purity.

WHEAT—Symbolic of the Resurrection.

WINGED MAN—Symbol ascribed to St. Matthew because his Gospel begins with the genealogy of Christ as a man.

X—Symbolizes Christ. This is the first letter of the Greek word for Christ.

X P—Signifies Jesus Christ.

ORTHODOX BAPTISMAL NAMES
(With name-day —New calendar)

MASCULINE

Abraham	Oct. 22	Gamaliel	Aug. 15	Matthias	Aug. 22
Achim	Aug. 14	George	May 6	Maurice	March 7
Adam	Jan. 27	Germain	May 25	Maximilian	Nov. 4
Adrian	Sept. 8	Gordian	Sept. 26	Michael	Sept. 19
Alexander	Sept. 12	Gregory	Feb. 7	Mitchell	Nov. 21
Alexis	March 30			Myron	Aug. 30
Ambrose	Dec. 20	Hadrian	Sept. 8		
Amos	June 28	Hermes	June 13	Nathan	May 5
Andrew	Dec. 13	Hilary	July 25	Nathaniel	June 24
Angus	March 22	Humphrey	June 25	Neil	Sept. 26
Anthony	Jan. 30			Nicholas	Dec. 19
Apollo	June 18	Ignatius	April 8		
Artemus	May 12	Igor	June 18	Obadiah	Dec. 2
Augustine	June 28	Isaac	Jan. 27	Olbian	May 17
		Isidore	May 27	Orestes	Dec. 26
Barnabas	June 24	Ivan	July 7	Orion	July 19
Barnaby	June 24				
Barry	Sept. 28	Jacob	Nov. 5	Paul	July 12
Barteus	June 24	James	May 13	Peter	July 12
Bartholomew	June 24	Jason	May 11	Philip	Nov. 27
Baruch	Sept. 28	Jeremy	May 14	Platon	April 18
Basil	Jan. 14	Jerome	June 28	Prosper	Sept. 6
Benedict	March 27	Joachim	Sept. 22		
Benjamin	Oct. 26	Joad	Sept. 22	Roman	Dec. 1
Bennett	March 27	Joe	April 17	Rufus	April 21
Blaise	Feb. 24	Joel	Nov. 1		
Boniface	Jan. 1	John	July 7	Samson	July 10
Boris	Aug. 6	Jonas	Nov. 18	Samuel	Sept. 2
		Joseph	Nov. 16	Serge	Oct. 20
Christian	May 22	Joshua	Sept. 14	Silas	Aug. 12
Christopher	May 22	Jude	July 2	Simeon	Feb. 16
Claude	June 16	Julian	July 4	Simon	May 23
Clement	Feb. 5	Julius	July 4	Spiridon	Dec. 25
Constantine	June 3	Justin	June 14	Stephen	Jan. 9
Cornelius	Sept. 26			Sylvester	Jan. 15
Cyril	May 24	Kay	June 14		
Cyrus	July 11	Kester	May 22	Terrence	Nov. 10
				Thaddeus	Sept. 3
Damian	July 14	Lawrence	Aug. 23	Theodore	May 5
Daniel	Dec. 30	Leander	Nov. 14	Thomas	Oct. 19
David	July 11	Leo	March 3	Timothy	Feb. 4
Demetrian	July 3	Leon	March 3	Titus	Sept. 7
Dennis	July 9	Leonidas	Aug. 21		
		Linus	Nov. 18	Urban	Nov. 13
Eleazer	Aug. 14	Lionel	March 3		
Elias	Aug. 2	Lucian	Oct. 28	Valentine	July 19
Emanuel	June 30	Lucius	June 14	Valerian	June 14
Emilian	Aug. 21	Luke	Oct. 31	Victor	Nov. 24
Ephraim	Feb. 10			Vincent	Nov. 24
Eugene	March 20	Magnus	May 12	Vladimir	July 28
		Manuel	June 30		
Fabius	Aug. 18	Mark	May 8	William	Jan. 14
Felix	July 19	Martin	April 27	Zachary	Sept. 18
Firmin	July 7	Matthew	Nov. 29	Zacheus	Dec. 1

ORTHODOX BAPTISMAL NAMES
(With name-day —New calendar)

FEMININE

Adrienne	Sept. 8	Eva	Jan. 4	Marilyn	April 14
Agatha	Feb. 18	Evelina	Jan. 4	Marjorie	Feb. 7
Agnes	July 18			Martha	June 22
Aileen	July 24	Faith	Sept. 30	Mary	April 14
Alexandra	May 6	Felecity	Feb. 14	Maude	Aug. 4
Amelia	Aug. 21			Maureen	May 16
Anastasia	Nov. 4	Georgia	May 6	May	Feb. 8
Angelina	Dec. 23	Georgiana	Jan. 11	Miriam	June 22
Anita	Dec. 22	Gladys	Jan. 6	Molly	April 14
Anna	Sept. 22			Muriel	Jan. 7
Anne	Nov. 16	Hannan	Sept. 22	Myrtle	Aug. 30
Annette	Aug. 7	Helen	June 3		
Antonia	June 26	Helena	June 3	Nadine	Sept. 30
Augusta	Dec. 7	Hermoine	Sept. 17	Nancy	Sept. 10
		Hester	Jan. 21	Naomi	Nov. 10
Barbara	Dec. 17	Hope	Sept. 30	Natalie	Sept. 8
Bernice	Oct. 17	Hulda	April 23	Nelly	June 3
Betsy	May 7	Hyacinth	July 16	Nina	Jan. 27
Betty	May 7				
Beulah	Feb. 19	Inez	July 18	Olga	July 24
		Irene	May 18	Olive	Aug. 7
Carita	June 14	Isabel	May 7		
Catherine	Dec. 7	Isadora	May 23	Paula	Feb. 23
Cecilia	Dec. 11			Pauline	Feb. 23
Charissa	April 29	Jane	July 7	Philippa	Nov. 27
Charity	Sept. 30	Janet	July 7	Phoebe	Sept. 16
Christine	Aug. 6	Jeanne	July 7	Priscilla	June 20
Claudette	May 31	Jenny	July 7	Prudence	April 28
Claudia	May 31	Joan	July 7		
Cornelia	Sept. 26	Joanna	July 10	Rachael	May 13
		Jocelyn	June 14	Rebecca	Oct. 22
Daria	April 1	Josephine	Nov. 16	Ruth	July 29
Darice	April 1	Judith	July 2		
Deborah	Sept. 28	Julia	July 29	Sally	Oct. 22
Dinah	May 13	Juliana	March 17	Sandra	May 6
Dolores	Jan. 8	June	May 30	Sarah	Oct. 22
Dora	Feb. 19			Sonia	Sept. 30
Dorcas	Feb. 19	Katherine	Dec. 7	Sophia	Sept. 30
Dorothy	Feb. 19	Kathleen	Dec. 7	Stephanie	Nov. 24
				Susan	Aug. 24
Edna	Sept. 30	Larissa	April 8	Susanna	Aug. 24
Effie	July 24	Laura	Aug. 31		
Eileen	July 24	Leah	Nov. 5	Tamara	May 14
Elaine	July 24	Leonie	March 3	Theodosia	June 11
Eleanor	July 24	Leonora	June 3	Theresa	Feb. 13
Elizabeth	Sept. 18	Lucia	Dec. 26		
Ellen	July 24	Lydia	April 5	Valentina	Feb. 23
Elsie	May 7			Valeria	June 19
Emilia	Aug. 21	Madeline	Aug. 4	Vera	Sept. 30
Emily	Aug. 21	Magdalene	Aug. 4	Veronica	April 15
Esther	Jan. 21	Marcia	May 8	Victoria	Nov. 23
Eugenia	Jan. 6	Margaret	Feb. 7	Vivien	April 1
Eunice	Nov. 10	Maria	April 14		
		Marian	Nov. 11	Xenia	Feb. 6

8

Bible References

BOOKS OF THE BIBLE

SUITABLE BIBLE PASSAGES

THE 23rd PSALM

THE LORD'S PRAYER

THE TEN COMMANDMENTS

THE BEATITUDES

THE CREED

FAITH, HOPE AND CHARITY

SYNOPSIS, BOOKS OF BIBLE

SYNOPSIS, APOCRYPHA

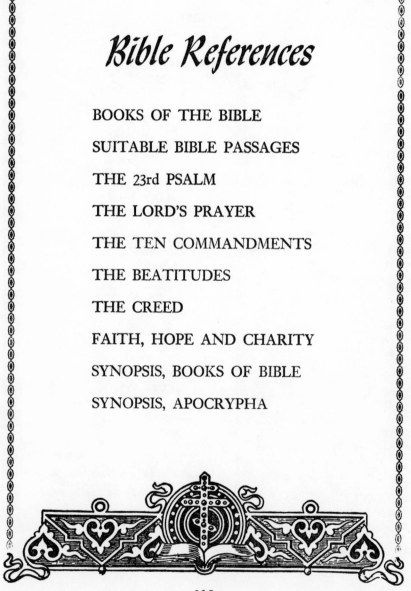

Books of the Bible

By reading three chapters daily and four chapters on Sundays, the entire Bible can be read in a year.

BIBLE PASSAGES SUITABLE FOR EVERY OCCASION

OLD TESTAMENT

Where the Ten Commandments are found—20th Chapter of Exodus or 5th Chapter of Deuteronomy.

For the Power of Prayer—II Kings, 6th verse of the 20th Chapter.

Two identical Bible Chapters—II Kings, Chapter 9 and Isaiah, Chapter 37.

Longest verse in the Bible—9th verse of Chapter 8 of Esther.

When you're discouraged, read the 40th Chapter of Isaiah.

For courage for your task, read the 1st Chapter of Joshua.

For a great invitation and a great opportunity, read the 55th Chapter of Isaiah.

For a prophet's viewpoint of worship that counts, read the first twelve verses of the 58th Chapter of Isaiah.

For a prophet's viewpoint of religion, read Isaiah, Chapter 1, 10th to 18th verses or Micah, Chapter 6, 6th to 8th verses.

For a marvelous description, read the 12th Chapter of Ecclesiastes.

PSALMS

To be reminded that sorrow and suffering follow forgetfulness of God, read the 137th Psalm.

Four identical verses in the Bible—107th Psalm, verses 8, 15, 21, 31.

When you're lonesome and fearful, turn to the Shepherd's Psalm, the 23rd Psalm.

When men fail you and for a renewed faith in God, read the 27th Psalm.

If you have sinned, read the 51st Psalm.

Before church services, read the 84th Psalm.

When you are in danger, read the 91st Psalm.

When you are despondent and blue, read the 34th Psalm.

If God seems far away, read the 139th Psalm.

If you have forgotten your blessings, read the 103rd Psalm.

When the world seems bigger than God, read the 90th Psalm.

When your prayers grow narrow and selfish, read the 67th Psalm.

Before you leave home for labor or travel, read the 121st Psalm.

To feel God's presence in nature, read the 24th Psalm.

For proof that the man who believes in God will triumph, read the 46th Psalm.

For a reminder that a good man will not spread slanders against his neighbor, read the 15th Psalm.

NEW TESTAMENT

Where the Lord's Prayer is found—6th Chapter of Matthew or 11th Chapter of Luke.

For Christ's idea of a Christian, read the Beatitudes, 5th Chapter of Matthew.

For the story of Paul's conversion, read the 9th Chapter of the Book of Acts.

Shortest verse in the Bible—John, 35th verse of Chapter 11.

For the story of the Prodigal Son, read the 15th Chapter of Luke.

To be fruitful, turn to the abiding chapter of the Bible, the 15th Chapter of John.

When you sorrow, seek solace by reading the 14th Chapter of John.

When you're worried, read the 19th through 34th verses of the 6th Chapter of Matthew.

When you're beset with doubts, read the 17th verse of the 7th Chapter of John.

For James' idea of religion, read the 19th through 27th verses of the 1st Chapter of James.

For the story of the Ten Virgins, read the 25th Chapter of Matthew.

When your faith needs stirring, read the 11th Chapter of Hebrews.

When you feel down and out, read the 31st through 39th verses of the 8th Chapter of Romans.

When you want peace and rest, read the 25th through 30th verses of the 11th Chapter of Matthew.

For Christian assurance, read the 1st through 30th verses of the 8th Chapter of Romans.

For Paul's secret of happiness, read the 12th through 17th verses of the 3rd Chapter of Colossians.

If you feel bitter or critical, read the 13th Chapter of I Corinthians, called by many Bible and literature scholars the most beautiful chapter in the Bible.

For Paul's idea of Christianity, read the 15th through 19th verses of the 5th Chapter of II Corinthians.

For Paul's rules for getting along with men, read the 12th Chapter of Romans. The first verse is called the consecration verse.

When you think of investments and returns, read the 17th through 31st verses of the 10th Chapter of Mark.

Greatest verse in the Bible—16th verse of the 3rd Chapter of John.

To find the Resurrection chapter of the Bible, turn to I Corinthians, Chapter 15.

The Rest verse of the Bible—Verse 28 of the 11th Chapter of Matthew.

The Last Commandment—Verse 8 of Chapter 1 of the Book of Acts.

Formulation of the Creed at the First Ecumenical Council held at Nicaea

The 23rd Psalm

(This beautiful passage, the most famous of the Psalms of David, is called the Shepherd's Psalm.)

The Lord is my shepherd; I shall not want.

He maketh me to lie down in green pastures;

He leadeth me beside the still waters.

He restoreth my soul.

He leadeth me in the paths of righteousness for His name's sake.

Yea, though I walk through the valley of the shadow of death,

I will fear no evil; for Thou art with me;

Thy rod and Thy staff they comfort me.

Thou preparest a table before me in the presence of mine enemies:

Thou anointest my head with oil; my cup runneth over.

Surely goodness and mercy shall follow me all the days of my life;

And I will dwell in the house of the Lord forever.

The Lord's Prayer

(During the Sermon on the Mount, Jesus taught His disciples how to pray, giving them the Lord's Prayer.)

Our Father, Who art in Heaven,

Hallowed be Thy Name;

Thy Kingdom come;

Thy will be done on earth as it is in Heaven.

Give us this day our daily bread.

And forgive us our trespasses,

As we forgive those who trespass against us.

And lead us not into temptation,

But deliver us from evil.

For Thine is the Kingdom,

And the Power,

And the Glory forever and ever.

AMEN

✝ ✝ ✝

The New Commandments of Jesus

Thou shalt love the Lord thy God with all thy heart, and with all thy soul, and with all thy strength, and with all thy mind; this is the first and great commandment. And the second is like unto it: Thou shalt love thy neighbor as thyself.

The Ten Commandments

Called God's ancient law, the Ten Commandments were given by God through Moses on Mount Sinai. Written on two tablets of stone, the commandments were divided with four on one tablet and six on the other. The first four regulate our relations to God and the other six regulate our relations with our fellow men.

1. I am the Lord thy God; Thou shalt have no other gods before Me.

2. Thou shalt not make unto thee any graven image or any likeness of anything that is in heaven above, or that is in the earth beneath, or that is in the water under the earth. Thou shalt not worship them, nor serve them.

3. Thou shalt not take the name of the Lord thy God in vain.

4. Remember the Sabbath day to keep it holy. Six days shalt thou labor and do all thy work; but the seventh day is the Sabbath of the Lord thy God.

5. Honor thy father and thy mother, that thy days may be long upon the land which the Lord thy God giveth thee.

6. Thou shalt not kill.

7. Thou shalt not commit adultery.

8. Thou shalt not steal.

9. Thou shalt not bear false witness against thy neighbor.

10. Thou shalt not covet thy neighbor's house, thou shalt not covet thy neighbor's wife, nor his manservant, nor his maidservant, nor his ox, nor his ass, nor anything that is thy neighbor's.

The Beatitudes

During the Sermon on the Mount, the most famous sermon ever delivered, Jesus gave the assembled multitude the Beatitudes— nine rules for happiness.

1. Blessed are the poor in spirit, for theirs is the Kingdom of Heaven.

2. Blessed are they that mourn; for they shall be comforted.

3. Blessed are the meek; for they shall inherit the earth.

4. Blessed are they that hunger and thirst for righteousness; for they shall be filled.

5. Blessed are the merciful; for they shall obtain mercy.

6. Blessed are the pure in heart; for they shall see God.

7. Blessed are the peacemakers; for they shall be called the children of God.

8. Blessed are they which are persecuted for righteousness' sake; for theirs is the Kingdom of Heaven.

9. Blessed are ye, when men shall revile you and persecute you, and shall say all manner of evil against you falsely for My sake. Rejoice and be exceedingly glad; for great is your reward in heaven.

MATTHEW 5:3-12

✝ ✝ ✝

In His Sermon on the Mount, Jesus also gave the people three other rules for righteous living.

"Seek ye first the Kingdom of God"

"Judge not that ye be not judged"

"Do unto others as ye would that they should do unto you"

This last precept has become known as the Golden Rule.

The Creed

The Nicene Creed was formulated at the first two Ecumenical Councils. At the first council, held in 325 A.D. at Nicaea, the first seven articles were adopted. The second council, which convened in 381 A.D. at Constantinople, added the last five articles of the Creed. The Creed expresses the belief of Orthodox worshipers.

I believe in One God, the Father Almighty, Maker of heaven and earth, and of all things visible and invisible.

And in one Lord Jesus Christ, the only begotten Son of God, begotten of the Father before all ages.

Light of Light, True God of True God, begotten, not created, being of one substance with the Father, through Whom all things were made.

Who for us men, and for our salvation, came down from heaven and was incarnate of the Holy Spirit and the Virgin Mary and became Man.

And was crucified for us under Pontius Pilate, and suffered, and was buried.

And rose again the third day according to the Scriptures.

And ascended into heaven and sitteth at the right hand of the Father.

And He shall come again with glory to judge the living and the dead.

And His kingdom shall have no end.

And I believe in the Holy Spirit, the Lord, the Giver of Life,

Who proceedeth from the Father, Who together with the Father and Son is worshiped and glorified. Who spake by the prophets.

And in One Holy, Catholic and Apostolic Church.

I acknowledge one Baptism for the remission of sins.

I look for the resurrection of the dead.

And the life in the world to come. AMEN

Faith, Hope and Charity

(This chapter is considered by many students of the Bible and literature as the most beautiful in the entire book.)

Though I speak with the tongues of men and of angels, and have not charity, I am become as sounding brass, or a tinkling cymbal.

And though I have the gift of prophecy, and understand all mysteries, and all knowledge; and though I have faith, so that I could remove mountains, and have not charity, I am nothing.

And though I bestow all my goods to feed the poor, and though I give my body to be burned, and have not charity, it profiteth me nothing.

Charity suffereth long, and is kind; charity envieth not; charity vaunted not itself, is not puffed up.

Doth not behave itself unseemly, seeketh not her own, is not easily provoked, thinketh no evil;

Rejoiceth not in iniquity, but rejoiceth in the truth;

Beareth all things, believeth all things, hopeth all things, endureth all things.

Charity never faileth; but whether there be prophecies, they shall fail; whether there be tongues, they shall cease; whether there be knowledge, it shall vanish away.

For we know in part, and we prophesy in part.

But when that which is perfect is come, then that which is in part shall be done away.

When I was a child, I spake as a child, I understood as a child, I thought as a child; but when I became a man, I put away childish things.

For now we see through a glass, darkly; but then face to face; now I know in part: but then shall I know even as also I am known.

And now abideth faith, hope, and charity, these three; but the greatest of these is charity.

I CORINTHIANS, Chapter 13

SYNOPSIS OF BOOKS OF THE BIBLE

OLD TESTAMENT

GENESIS . . . Creation of the world—The garden of Eden—Adam and Eve—Man's disobedience, sin and punishment—Cain and Abel; the murder of Abel—Birth of Seth—Genealogy of the patriarchs—The world's wickedness—Noah, the ark and the flood—The rainbow, God's promise—Generations of Noah—Tower of Babel—Abraham, first of God's chosen people—Battle of the kings—Sarah, Hagar and Ishmael—Destruction of Sodom and Gomorrah—Isaac and Abraham's offering—Death of Sarah—Rebecca, Isaac's wife—Esau and Jacob—Jacob's vision—Jacob's children—Covenant between Jacob and Laban—Jacob and Esau reconciled—Death of Isaac—Joseph sold by his brothers—Joseph cast into prison in Egypt—Joseph interprets Pharaoh's dreams—Famine in Egypt—Joseph's brothers visit him—Joseph meets his father—Jacob blesses his sons—Burial of Jacob—Death of Joseph. (Author . . . Moses.)

EXODUS . . . Birth of Moses—Moses sent to deliver Israel—God's message to Pharaoh—The rod becomes a serpent—The ten plagues—Israelites leave Egypt—Passage through the Red Sea—The Ten Commandments received on Mt. Sinai—Various laws and ordinances—The priesthood—Ark of the covenant—Aaron's golden calf—The tabernacle. (Author . . . Moses.)

LEVITICUS . . . Laws of offerings—Aaron and his sons consecrated to priesthood—Slaying of Nadab and Abihu—Clean and unclean things—Laws of leprosy—Aaron's sin offering—Unlawful marriages—Feasts of the Lord—The year of jubilee—Vows and their redemption. (Author . . . Moses.)

NUMBERS . . . The twelve tribes numbered—Families, number and charge of the Levites—Service of the Levites—The trial of jealousy—Law of the Nazarites—Offerings of the princes—Journey from Sinai to Paran—Seventy elders appointed—Sedition of Miriam and Aaron—Evil report of the spies—Laws of offerings—Punishment for breaking the Sabbath—Plague of fiery serpents—Balak and Balaam—All Israel numbered—Two and forty journeys of the Israelites. (Author . . . Moses.)

DEUTERONOMY . . . Israel's history by Moses—Conquest of Canaan—Exhortation to obedience—Cities of refuge—The Ten Commandments—Idolatry forbidden—Various laws and ordinances—Song of Moses—God's charge to Joshua—Death and burial of Moses. (Author . . . Moses. Last chapter added by another.)

JOSHUA . . . Rahab and the spies—People pass over Jordan—Downfall of Jericho—Death of Achan—The crafty Gibeonites—Sun and moon stand still—Kings conquered by Joshua—The cities of Judah—The land divided—Cities given to the Levites—Death and burial of Joshua. (Author . . . Joshua. Last verses added by another.)

JUDGES . . . The heathen in the land—An angel rebukes the people—Nations left to prove Israel—Deborah and Barak deliver Israel—Jael kills Sisera—Song of Deborah and Barak—Exploits of Gideon—Conspiracy of Abimelech

—Jephtha and his rash vow—Angel appears to Manoah—History of Samson—The Benjamites smitten. (Author . . . Unknown, probably Samuel.)

RUTH . . . Misfortunes of Elimelech—Ruth cleaves to Naomi—Ruth gleans in the field of Boaz—Boaz shows Ruth great favor—Ruth at the feet of Boaz—Boaz marries Ruth. (Author . . . Unknown, probably Samuel.)

I SAMUEL . . . Hannah's prayer—Birth of Samuel—Hannah's song of thanksgiving—The ministry of Samuel—Destruction of Dagon—Israel desires a king—Saul annointed by Samuel—Jonathan smites the Philistines—Saul rejected for disobedience—Saul kills Azag—David slays Goliath—Friendship of Jonathan and David—Envy of Saul—Saul seeks to kill David—Death of Samuel—Saul consults witch of Endor—Saul and his sons slain. (Author . . . Samuel. Completed by Nathan and Gad.)

II SAMUEL . . . David becomes king of Judah—Battle of Gibeon—David mourns for Abner—David becomes king of Israel—Ark brought to Jerusalem—David's great transgression—Uriah slain—Parable of Nathan—Birth of Solomon—Rebellion of Absalom—Death of Absalom—Civil dissension in the kingdom—Seven sons of Saul hanged—David's mighty men. (Authors . . . Nathan and Gad.)

I KINGS . . . Solomon annointed king—Solomon asks wisdom of the Lord—Solomon judges between two women—Solomon's greatness—King Hiram's message—Building of Solomon's temple—Dedication of the temple—Solomon builds cities—Visit of Queen of Sheba—Idolatry of Jeroboam—Wicked reign of Ahab—Elijah fed by ravens—Elijah raises widow's son—Baal's prophets confounded—Mantle of Elijah falls on Elisha—Naboth's vineyard—Death of Ahab. (Author . . . Unknown, probably Jeremiah.)

II KINGS . . . Elisha brings fire from heaven—Elisha raises Shunammite's son—Naaman cured of leprosy—Jezebel slain—The temple repaired—Last events in history of Israel—The good reign of Hezekiah—Babylonian captivity. (Author . . . Unknown, probably Jeremiah.)

I CHRONICLES . . . Genealogy of the sons of Israel—Families of the Levites—Cities of the priests—David's mighty men—Summary of events during the reign of David. (Author . . . Attributed to Ezra.)

II CHRONICLES . . . Solomon's strength and wealth—Summary of the account of the building of the temple—Ark brought into the holy place—Death of Solomon—History of the southern kingdom—Burning of the temple—The Jewish captivity. (Author . . . Attributed to Ezra.)

EZRA . . . Proclamation of Cyrus for building the temple—Number of people returning from Babylon—The temple's foundation laid—Adversaries attempt to hinder the work—The temple completed—Feast of the Passover—Commission of Artaxerxes to Ezra—Ezra's prayer and confession of sins—The people separated from strange wives. (Author . . . Ezra.)

NEHEMIAH . . . Feasting and prayer of Nehemiah—Commission to rebuild Jerusalem—Names of those building the wall—Work continued despite scoffers—the work finished—Genealogy of those returning from Babylon—Gifts of the people—Feast of tabernacles—Prayer of the Levites—Points of the covenant—Dedication of the walls. (Author . . . Nehemiah.)

ESTHER . . . Queen Vashti refuses to attend feast of Ahasuerus—New queen to be chosen—Esther preferred as queen—Haman's advancement—Esther's feast—Esther accuses Haman—Haman hanged—Jews victorious over enemies—Feast of purim instituted. (Author . . . Ascribed to Ezra. Possibly written by Mordecai.)

JOB . . . Riches and virtues of Job—Job's trials and patience—Tempted by Satan, Job curses day of birth—Eliphaz teaches God's judgments are for the wicked, not the righteous—Happy end of God's correction—Justice of God in dealing with men shown by Bildad—Afflictions no proof of guilt—God's wisdom declared unsearchable by Zophar—State and portion of the wicked—Job protests his integrity—The greatness of God's works—God's mighty works—Job humbles himself—Job's captivity ended and his happy state restored. (Author . . . Unknown, attributed to Elihu.)

PSALMS . . . A collection of 150 spiritual songs or poems, many of them being set to music for Tabernacle and Temple worship. The book of Psalms is divided into five sections, each ending with a doxology—The six psalms, 113th to 118th are the Passover psalms—three sung before and three after the Passover—The 120th to 134th are processional psalms, sung by pilgrims going up to the feasts—The five final psalms are the Hallelujah psalms, all beginning with "Praise the Lord"— The Psalms cover varied subjects—praise, thanksgiving, prayer, historical, instructive and prophetic—including prophetic psalms on the crucifixion, resurrection, ascension and the extension of Christ's kingdom. (Authors . . . David wrote 73; Sons of Korah, 11; Asaph, 12; Hezekiah, 10; Moses, one; Heman, one; Ethan, one; and the rest anonymous.)

PROVERBS . . . Benefits of wisdom—Exhortation to obedience—Blessings of faith, contentment and chastity—Custom and error of folly—Moral virtues and their contrary vices—Various maxims and wise observations of Solomon. (Authors . . . Some written by Solomon, others selected by him. Later additions long afterward by men of Hezekiah.)

ECCLESIASTES . . . Preacher shows all is vanity—Nothing is better than joy in our labor—A season for everything—Vanity increased by vices—Riches are worthless without use—Remedies against vanity—A good name, mortification, patience, wisdom—Similar things happen to all—Observations on wisdom and folly—God's providence rules over all—Poetic picture of old age—Conclusion, God alone satisfies. (Author . . . Solomon.)

SONG OF SOLOMON . . . The fair bride and the adorable bridegroom—The church's great delight in her Lord—Mutual love of Christ and his church—Christ shows the graces of the church and his love toward her—Additional similes to show the mutual love between the bridegroom and bride—This book a mysterious allegory. (Author . . . Solomon.)

ISAIAH . . . Five prophetic discourses directed to the Jews and Ephraimites—Rebellion of Judah—Coming of Christ's kingdom—Prophetic discourses on the fate of many nations—Isaiah's vision—Judgments on Judah—Afflictions to idolaters—The fall of Assyria—Triumph of Israel over Babylon—The judgment of Moab—Overthrow of Tyre—Discourses denouncing judgments on disobedience of Jews and consoling true followers of God—God's care over his vineyard—The promise of Christ's coming—Blessings of Christ's kingdom—Prayer and song of thanksgiving of Hezekiah—Discourses referring to the Messiah and the deliverance of the Jews from Babylon—Christ sent to the Gentiles—The passion, crucifixion and glory of the Messiah. (Author . . . Isaiah.)

JEREMIAH . . . God expostulates with the Jews—Promises to the penitent —Judgments on the Jews—Jeremiah laments the sins of the people—The prophet's supplication—God's covenant—Exhortation to repentance—Ruin of the Jews predicted—Blessings of trust in God—False prophets denounced—Good and bad figs—Conquests of Nebuchadnezzar—Letters to the captives in Babylon—Gracious restoration of Israel—Jeremiah in prison—The branch of righteousness—Destruction of Jerusalem foretold—Jerusalem captured—Zedekiah blinded and sent to Babylon—Conspiracy of Ismael—Conquest of Egypt foretold—Judgments on Moab, Edom, Damascus and Babylon—Jerusalem besieged and captured. (Author . . . Jeremiah.)

LAMENTATIONS . . . A book of pathetic compositions deploring the fulfillment of the prophecies already uttered by Jeremiah—The miserable estate of Jerusalem—The faithful bewail their calamities—Pitiful complaint of Zion in prayer to God. (Author . . . Jeremiah.)

EZEKIEL . . . Denunciations against the Jewish people mixed with promises of restoration—Vision of four cherubims and the glory of God—Type of the prophet's hair—Type of a chain—Sun worshippers—Vision of the coals of fire—Vision of the wheels—Captivity of Zedekiah—Reproof of lying prophets and idolaters—God's love toward Jerusalem—Parable of two eagles and a vine —Unjust parable of sour grapes—Parable of lion's whelps—The sharp and bright sword—Listing of sins in Jerusalem—The boiling pot—Prophecies against the Tyrians and Sidonians—Promise of deliverance to the Jews and their restoration to their own land—Conquest of Egypt by Nebuchadnezzar predicted—Israel's victory over Gog and Magog—Vision of new temple, new city and new government typical of a universal church filled with the glory of God. (Author . . . Ezekiel.)

DANIEL . . . The dream of Nebuchadnezzar and its interpretation—Daniel's advancement—Miraculous preservation and promotion of Shadrach, Meshach and Abed-nego—A second dream of Nebuchadnezzar interpreted and fulfilled—Belshazzar's feast—Handwriting on the wall and its meaning—The kingdom taken by the Medes and Persians—Delivery of Daniel from the lion's den—Vision of the four beasts—Vision of the ram and he-goat—The seventy weeks foretold—The invasion and tyrany of the Romans. (Author . . . Daniel.)

HOSEA . . . The idolatry of the people—Desolation of Israel—God's judgment against the people and priests—Exhortation to repentance—Reproof of manifold sins—Israel's distress and captivity—Threats against impiety and idolatry—Prophetic declaration of the restoration of all the tribes—Separation of the tribes from idols and the glory of the latter days. (Author . . . Hosea.)

JOEL . . . Joel exhorts the people to mourn for their sins—God's terrible judgments—Zion comforted—The Spirit to be poured out on all flesh—The judgments of God against the enemies of the church. (Author . . . Joel.)

AMOS . . . The necessity of God's judgments—Complaints against unthankfulness—Reproof of idolatry and oppression—The hardness of heart of Israel—Lamentation for Israel—Judgments averted by prayer of Amos—A basket of summer fruit—The restoration of the tabernacle of David. (Author . . . Amos.)

OBADIAH . . . Judgments denounced on the Edomites—The pride and injustice of Edom—The restoration and future prosperity of the Jews. (Author . . . Obadiah.)

JONAH . . . First visit to Nineveh by Jonah—Jonah betrayed by a tempest and cast into the sea—Jonah's prayer—Jonah delivered from the great fish—Second visit to Nineveh by Jonah—Jonah preaches to the Ninevites—Jonah rebuked by a gourd for his repinings. (Author . . . Jonah.)

MICAH . . . Jacob exhorted to mourn for idolatry—Reproof of injustice and oppression—The glory of the church—Christ's birth and kingdom—The triumph of the church over her enemies. (Author . . . Micah.)

NAHUM . . . The goodness of God to his people—Victorious armies against Nineveh—Miserable ruin of the bloody city. (Author . . . Nahum.)

HABAKKUK . . . Appeal to God on account of impiety and vice—The approaching captivity as a punishment for wickedness—Future deliverance through the promised Messiah—The just live by faith—Babylonian empire's destruction foretold—Prayer for prompt help for Israel. (Author . . . Habakkuk.)

ZEPHANIAH . . . The sins of Judah bring severe judgments—Jerusalem reproved sharply—Waiting for the restoration of Israel. (Author . . . Zephaniah.)

HAGGAI . . . Building of the temple urged—Reward of abundant harvest—Mighty revolution by Christ's kingdom prophesied—The glory of the later house to surpass that of the former. (Author . . . Haggai.)

ZECHARIAH . . . Vision of horses—Redemption of Zion—Christ's coming promised—The golden candlestick—The flying roll—The four chariots—Temple and kingdom of Christ, the Branch—Cause of the captivity—Good works required of the Jews—God defends his church—Christ's care of his flock—The coming of the Messiah. (Author . . . Zechariah.)

MALACHI . . . The divine displeasure against sin—Coming of Christ and ministry of his forerunner, John the Baptist—Judgments to accompany the coming of the Messiah—Separation of the righteous from the wicked—Appearance of the Sun of Righteousness. (Author . . . Malachi.)

NEW TESTAMENT

St. Matthew . . . Genealogy of Christ—Visit of the wise men to Bethlehem—Children slain by Herod's order—Flight into Egypt—Jesus at Nazareth—Preaching of John the Baptist—Temptation of Christ—Christ heals the diseased—Sermon on the mount—Faith of the centurion—Various miracles—The twelve Apostles sent out—Christ bears witness to John—Pharisees reproved—Parables concerning the kingdom of God—John the Baptist beheaded—Feeding the multitude—Transfiguration of Christ—Teachings of Jesus—Christ in Jerusalem—Various parables—Rulers conspire against Christ—Christ's agony in the garden—Christ delivered to Pilate—Christ condemned, crucified and buried—The resurrection of Christ—Appearances to disciples. (Author . . . Matthew.)

St. Mark . . . Baptism and temptation of Christ—Healing of many who were diseased—The twelve Apostles chosen—Sin against the Holy Spirit—Parable of the sower—Christ stills the tempest—Legion of devils cast out—Other miracles—Christ walks on the sea—Sight restored to the blind—Christ foretells his death—Christ blesses children—Various warnings and exhortations—The arguments of the Sadducees proven wrong by Christ—Lord's Supper instituted—Christ's crucifixion—Appearances to disciples after resurrection. (Author . . . Mark.)

St. Luke . . . Prophecy of Elizabeth and Mary concerning Christ—Birth of John the Baptist—Christ's birth foretold—Prophecy of Zacharias—Nativity of Jesus—Simeon and Anna prophesy—Christ questions the doctors in the temple—The miraculous draught of fishes—Matthew the publican called—Love to enemies advocated—Christ's testimony to John—Women minister to Christ—Many miracles performed by Christ—The good Samaritan—Discourses to disciples by Christ—Parable of the prodigal son—Parable of the rich man and Lazarus—The widow's mite—Christ denied by Peter—Christ betrayed by Judas—The crucifixion, death and burial of Christ—Christ's resurrection and ascension. (Author . . . Luke.)

St. John . . . The divinity and humanity of Christ—The marriage in Cana—Christ purges the temple—Discourse to Nicodemus—Discourse to the woman of Samaria—Jesus performs miracles—Christ declares who he is—Raising Lazarus from the dead—Christ in Jerusalem—Jesus washes his disciple's feet—Christ's last discourses to his disciples—Death of Christ by crucifixion, his burial and resurrection—Christ's charge to Peter. (Author . . . John.)

Acts of the Apostles . . . First Pentecost after Christ's resurrection and events preceding it—Acts at Jerusalem and in Judea and Samaria among the Christians—Acts in Caesarea and the receiving of Gentiles—First journey of Paul and Barnabas among the Gentiles—Second journey of Paul and Barnabas—First journey to Rome by Paul—Paul's shipwreck—Paul preaching in Rome. (Author . . . Luke.)

Romans . . . Jews and Gentiles alike under condemnation—Justification by faith—Peace with God through faith—Dominion of the law—Calling of the

Gentiles—God has not cast off Israel—Various exhortations—Brotherly charity —Paul's success in his labors—Paul's salutations to his fellow helpers. (Author . . . Paul.)

I CORINTHIANS . . . The foolishness of preaching—Christ the only foundation—Answers to questions concerning civil law, marriage, meats offered to idols and Christian liberty—Warning against idolatry—The place of women in the church—The Lord's Supper—Spiritual gifts—Praises of charity—The resurrection—Friendly admonitions and greetings. (Author . . . Paul.)

II CORINTHIANS . . . Christians encouraged—The law and the gospels— The apostle declares his ministry—Effect of Godly sorrow—Liberality and thanksgiving—The apostle excuses his self-boasting—The apostle glories in his infirmities—Obstinate sinners threatened. (Author . . . Paul.)

GALATIANS . . . The gospel is not of men but of God—Justification by faith, not works—All believers justified—Freed by Christ from the law, we are no longer servants of it—Allegory of Agar and Sara—Liberty of the gospel— Fruit of the Spirit—Exhortation to well doing. (Author . . . Paul.)

EPHESIANS . . . Greeting and thanksgiving—Election and adoption—Salvation of the Gentiles—The great love of Christ—Considerations which should impel all believers to Christian unity—Various ministries in the church—Mutual duties of husbands and wives—Duties of children toward parents—Duties of servants toward their masters—The Christian's armor. (Author . . . Paul.)

PHILIPPIANS . . . The apostle expresses his thankfulness for the fruits of faith among the Philippians—Ready to glorify Christ by life or death—Indifference to imprisonment and suffering—Unity and humbleness of mind commended—Warning against false teachers and carnal Christians—The apostle's efforts to gain holiness—General exhortations. (Author . . . Paul.)

COLOSSIANS . . . The true Christ—Men urged to receive Christ—Constancy in Christ required—Charity, humility and other duties—For a blameless and holy life, fervent prayer necessary. (Author . . . Paul.)

I THESSALONIANS . . . Thanksgiving for the grace received by the Thessalonians—Sincerity and love of the apostle and his fellow-workers—Effect produced by their preaching—Desire, care and joy on account of the converts—Exhortations to grow in holiness and brotherly love—Concerning those who shall meet Christ at his coming—Concerning the times. (Author . . . Paul.)

II THESSALONIANS . . . Thanksgiving and prayer for the Thessalonians— Doctrine concerning the man of sin—Thessalonians comforted against this trial—Directions to correct the disorderly—Various precepts. (Author . . . Paul.)

I TIMOTHY . . . Instructions to Timothy—Legalizing teachers—Confirmation of the gospel exemplified in the apostle—Directions relative to prayer and good works—Qualifications of a bishop—Duties of deacons—Timothy's personal conduct and pastoral duties—Concerning servants, false teachers and riches. (Author . . . Paul.)

II TIMOTHY . . . Commendation of Timothy's faith—Exhortation to Christian fortitude—Fidelity and generosity of Onesiphorus to Paul—Directions for avoiding things leading to apostasy—Declentions will come—Paul's rejoicing in view of immediate death. (Author . . . Paul.)

TITUS . . . Instructions for Titus to ordain good presbyters—To reprove and admonish the Cretans, taking care to set himself as an example of good works—To avoid foolish questions and shun heretics. (Author . . . Paul.)

PHILEMON . . . The apostle rejoices at the faith and love of Philemon—Appeals for Onesimus, who had been converted and sent back by Paul, to be forgiven and received kindly. (Author . . . Paul.)

HEBREWS . . . A demonstration of the superiority of the gospel dispensation—Christ more worthy than Moses—Christ's priesthood—Priesthoods of Christ and Aaron compared—Perfection of the blood and sacrifice of Christ—The weakness of the law sacrifices—Worthy fruits of faith—Various admonitions for holy living. (Author . . . Unknown. Attributed to Paul or Barnabas.)

JAMES . . . Patience in enduring outward and conquering inward temptations—Hearing the word to be joined with practice—Respect of persons—Exhortation to universal benevolence—Inefficiency of faith without works—Sins to be avoided—Patience in afflictions—Doom of wicked rich men. (Author . . . James, the Just.)

I PETER . . . Exhortation to holiness—Christ the sure foundation—Exhortations to obedience, unity and love—Duty of wives and husbands—Christian virtues commended. (Author . . . Peter.)

II PETER . . . Great promises for believers—Constancy in the faith—False teachers described and denounced—Certainty of Christ's coming to judgment. (Author . . . Peter.)

I JOHN . . . Christ our propitiation—Sins of infirmity—False teachers—Great love of God—Eternal life. (Author . . . John.)

II JOHN . . . Love manifesting itself in a life of obedience—False teachers to be shunned. (Author . . . John.)

III JOHN . . . Commendation of piety and hospitality—Exhortation to follow only the good. (Author . . . John.)

JUDE . . . Christians exhorted to hold fast the profession of their faith. (Author . . . Jude.)

REVELATION . . . Introduction describing the circumstances of writing the message—Messages to the seven churches of Asia—Vision of the living creatures and the elders—Judgments confronting evil—The seals, trumpets and vials—Two martyred witnesses—Woman crowned with the sun; her child the victim of the dragon and two wild beasts—Enemies of the child meet their doom—The new heaven and the new earth—Coming of Christ—Pure river of the water of life. (Author . . . John).

THE APOCRYPHA

The original Septuagint version of the Bible, named from the seventy scholars who worked on the translation into Greek, included books not found in modern standard Bibles. These books, collectively called the Apocrypha, are termed Deutercanonical (secondary) and theological authorities regard them as semi-canonical; good and useful books but below the standard of other books of the Bible. The books of the Apocrypha originated in the first to third centuries, B.C., but were never included in the Hebrew Old Testament. The Eastern Orthodox Church recognizes these books.

SYNOPSIS OF BOOKS OF THE APOCRYPHA

II EZRA (Often called Ezdras, the Greek form of Ezra) . . . This book is a continuation of the book of Ezra. It includes compilations from Ezra, II Chronicles and Nehemiah. Contains stories about Zerubbabel, governor of Judaea during the rebuilding of the temple. He had great influence in bringing the second temple into being. Sacred vessels taken from Jerusalem by Nebuchadnezzar at the time of the captivity are restored. The book also includes the story of the three youths. Object of this book is to picture the tolerance of Darius and Cyrus towards the Jews.

III EZRA (Ezdras) . . . Contains visions given to Ezra regarding God's government of the universe. The tragic fate of the Jews after the destruction of Jerusalem is lamented along with God's failure to reward the righteous. Assurance is given through visions of a mourning mother, the eagle and the Son of Man that God would manifest his justice through a four-hundred-year rule of the Messiah, the resurrection and judgment. The conversion of heathen nations under one shepherd is predicted. Ezra restores the sacred books, including certain lost scriptures, and places the Old Testament books in their proper order.

TOBIT . . . Tobit, a pious man of the tribe of Naphtali, is exiled to Nineveh. He observed the law but was blinded after burying a dead Jew. Tobias, the son of Tobit, brought back to Nineveh ten talents of silver lent to Gabael by Tobit and restored his father's sight with the gill of a fish caught in the Tigris river. Tobias, guided by the angel Raphael, had previously driven away the demon Asmodeus and married Sara. The message of the book: God never forsakes those who trust in him and keep his commandments. Tobit praises the Lord for many kindnesses.

JUDITH . . . A historical romance relating the heroic deed of Judith, a rich, beautiful and devout Jewish widow living in the days of the Babylonian invasion of Judah. Nebuchadnezzar sent Holophernes to punish the Jews for failing to provide troops in his successful campaign against the king of Media. Judith assured the Jews the Lord would deliver them. She enticed Holophernes, after going to his tent, and then cut off his head to save the city. She praised the Lord and lived happily afterwards.

WISDOM OF SOLOMON . . . Similar in parts to the book of Job and to Proverbs and Ecclesiastes. Includes the rewards of wisdom. The ungodly Jews enjoy the pleasures of the world while persecuting the pious and needy. After death, the ungodly will repent in vain while the righteous enjoy eternal bliss. This book expounds on the nature of wisdom and how to attain it. It contrasts the heroes of wisdom, from Adam to Moses, with the wicked and also cites the contrast between Israelites and Egyptians. The Lord loves those living in wisdom. Pagan worship is foolish. Solomon obtained wisdom from God, a reflection of God's glory.

WISDOM OF THE SON OF SIRACH (also called ECCLESIASTICUS) . . . This book is similar to the book of Proverbs. Wisdom is obtained from observing God's laws. A great many subjects are treated, including the honoring of parents, humility, kindness, tests and rewards of wisdom, wrong conduct, the search for wisdom, the blessings of wisdom, good and bad wives, troubles and sins of rich men, the education of children, table manners, the father as ruler of the household, dreams, travel, true piety, mourning, and the value of higher education. This book praises a long list of Old Testament notables and gives the prayer of the Son of Sirach. Main message of the book: rules of conduct for social, religious and domestic living.

BARUCH . . . The Jews are admonished to repent after the destruction of Jerusalem. Baruch informs the suffering Jews that all their misfortunes were sent by God because they were sinful. This book includes a poem in praise of wisdom and a prayer to God for mercy. Addressed mainly to exiles, it tells the Jews to be comforted in the expected early return of exiles and the destruction of Babylon. Baruch, a scribe of Jeremiah, paraphrases Jeremiah, Daniel and other prophets.

JEREMIAH . . . This book is a message sent to captives in Babylon—a warning against Babylon idolatry. It states that God's angel is with them and is protecting their souls. The Jews are told that God punished them for their sins with seventy years of captivity in Babylon. Somewhat sarcastic in vein, this book denounces the folly of idolatry.

I MACCABEES . . . A historical work covering events during the historic struggle of the Jews for freedom. It is one of the best sources of Jewish history for the period of 175-135 B.C. The Maccabees were leaders of the Jewish people, five sons of the priest Mattatias (Judas, Simon, Jonathan, Eleazar and John). The book begins with a background and beginnings of the rebellion and continues with a poem praising Judas Maccabees. It relates the wars of Judas for religious liberty and his defeating Nicanor. Jonathan is forced to sign a treaty with Bacchides, at first allying himself with Demetrius but later turning against both of them. Simon supported Demetrius and made Judaea independent and consolidated the power. He defied an ultimatum from Antiochus VII but was later assassinated.

II MACCABEES . . . Letters from Palestine to Egyptian Jews telling of the rededication of the temple in 164 B.C. This book tells of the Maccabean struggles, mainly in the period of 175–161 B.C. and is purported to be a summary of five books of Jason of Cyrene. Also covered are the initial victories of Judas Maccabees, plundering of the temple, and the heroic sufferings of the Jews as they defended their religious heritage and their customs. Maccabees II is inferior to Maccabees I.

III MACCABEES . . . Centers around two miraculous events—an account of the refusal of admission to King Ptolomy Philopater into the Jerusalem temple's sanctuary and the dramatic rescue of the Jews from extermination by elephants at Alexandria.

149

9

Orthodox Calendar

THE JULIAN CALENDAR

HOLY DAYS AND FAST DAYS

DAILY CYCLE OF SERVICES

GREAT LENT AND EASTER DATES

EPISTLE AND GOSPEL TEXTS

DEDICATED DAYS OF THE YEAR

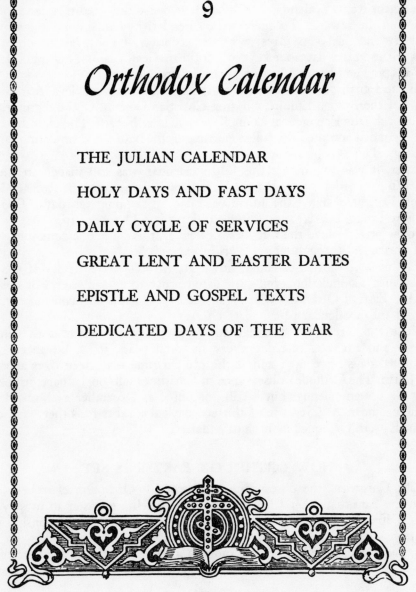

THE JULIAN CALENDAR

Eastern Orthodox churches regulate the church calendar according to the old Julian calendar which often proves confusing, especially to younger members of the Church who are puzzled about the differences in dates between Eastern Orthodox Church date observances and the dates observed by other church denominations. Christmas and Easter, as observed in Eastern Orthodox churches, loom especially prominent because of their difference in dates from other churches. A brief explanation of the differences between the Julian and Gregorian calendars is given here.

In the year 46 B.C., Julius Caesar, the Roman Emperor, decided to correct the ancient Roman calendar which had become so distorted that January was falling in the autumn. To correct the calendar, he had the months adjusted to thirty and thirty-one days with the exception of February which had 28 days with an extra day added every four years (leap year). This new calendar was adopted and became known as the Julian calendar.

In the fourth century, during the reign of Constantine the Great as Emperor of the Roman Empire, the first Christian Council of the dignitaries of the church (the Ecumenical Council) was held at Nicaea. The church leaders at this council accepted the Julian calendar as the basis for formulating church holidays. This was passed in 325 A.D.

Later, it was found that the Julian calendar was still inaccurate and in 1562 A.D., on orders of the Roman Pope Gregory the 13th, the Roman Council of Trident changed the Julian calendar by skipping ten days. This was done by calling the day that followed Thursday, October 4th, 1562, Friday, October 15th. Named the Gregorian calendar, this is the one commonly used in America and throughout the world today.

The new Gregorian calendar, however, violated certain rules of the first Ecumenical Council concerning the date for determining Easter. For this reason the Eastern Orthodox Church refused to adopt it and continued to use the old Julian calendar to calculate church days.

Since the Gregorian calendar advanced ten days in the 16th century (1562) and advances one day every hundred years, it has advanced three additional days since 1562 and at the present time is thirteen days ahead of the Julian. The Orthodox observance of Christmas falls on January 7th on the new Gregorian calendar but is still computed as December 25th on the old Julian calendar. A difference of thirteen days also exists for other fixed dates of the Eastern Orthodox Church calendar.

HOW ORTHODOX EASTER IS SET

Like Christmas, the observance of Easter by Orthodox churches varies from the date that other Christian churches celebrate Easter in most years. This is due not only to calendar differences but also to the relationship with the Jewish Passover.

In many ancient calendars, the months were set by the appearance of the new crescent moon in the western sky. That was true of the Hebrew calendar and it was one of the duties of the priests to watch for a new moon and announce the new month by blowing a horn.

Since the time elapsing between the return of the same phase of the moon is twenty-nine and a half days, the Hebrews alternated the length of their months between twenty-nine and thirty days.

The first month of the old ecclesiastical calendar of the Jews is the month of Nisan which begins with the new moon occurring about the time of the vernal equinox, the beginning of spring.

The 14th of Nisan marks the beginning of the holy season of the Jewish Passover, commemorating the sparing of the Hebrews in Egypt when God, smiting the first born in Egyptian homes, passed over the houses of the Children of Israel whose doorposts were marked by sprinkling them with the blood of a lamb.

During this period of the Jewish year, Jesus was crucified. The Last Supper, of which Christ partook, with his twelve disciples, was the Feast of the Passover. Therefore, the Jewish Passover and the Christian Easter are closely connected.

The rule for determining the date for Easter was set by the Council of Nicaea in 325 A.D. The Jewish Passover, coming fourteen days after the beginning of the month of Nisan, comes at full moon and may fall on any day of the week. The Council decided that Easter should always fall on a Sunday, the one following the Paschal (or Passover) full moon which was also the first full moon of the vernal equinox.

The Council of Nicaea also wanted to keep Easter forever separated from the Jewish Passover, so it was decided that when the full moon and the Passover itself came on a Sunday, the Christian Easter would be observed a week later. Easter in the Eastern Orthodox churches is never celebrated before the Jewish Passover because Christ Himself observed the Passover at the Last Supper before His betrayal.

The Easter observed under the Gregorian calendar is set by calculations which take in other factors besides lunar calculations to account for additional differences in the observance of Easter.

IMPORTANT HOLY DAYS AND FAST DAYS

*CHRISTMAS—
NATIVITY OF THE SAVIOUR ...... December 25 (January 7)

DAY BEFORE EPIPHANY .... January 5 (January 18)

*EPIPHANY—BAPTISM OF JESUS .... January 6 (January 19)
(Manifestation of the Most Holy Trinity
Great Blessing of Waters)

*MEETING OF JESUS BY ST. SIMEON .... February 2 (February 15)
(Fortieth Day After the Birth of Christ
Purification—Blessing of Candles)

*ANNUNCIATION OF THE VIRGIN MARY ... March 25 (April 7)

GREAT LENT—A moveable Lenten period observed for 7 weeks (48
days) preceding Easter

*PALM SUNDAY—Entry of the Lord into Jerusalem. Sunday before Easter

**EASTER—The Feast of Feasts—Falls on the Sunday following the Spring
full moon

*ASCENSION—Forty days after Easter. Always falls on a Thursday

*PENTECOST—Fifty days after Easter. Always falls on a Sunday

ST. PETER'S LENT—A moveable Lenten period preceding St. Peter and
Paul's Day.

NATIVITY OF JOHN THE FORERUNNER
(John the Baptist) ....June 24 (July 7)

ST. PETER AND PAUL'S DAY .... June 29 (July 12)

ASSUMPTION LENT—A fifteen-day Lenten period preceding the AS-
SUMPTION OF THE VIRGIN MARY

*TRANSFIGURATION OF THE LORD ...... August 6 (August 19)

*ASSUMPTION OF THE VIRGIN MARY....August 15 (August 28)

DAY OF ST. JOHN'S MARTYRDOM
(Beheading of John the Baptist) .... August 29 (September 11)

*NATIVITY OF THE VIRGIN MARY .. September 8 (September 21)

*ELEVATION OF THE HOLY CROSS..September 14 (September 27)

CHRISTMAS LENT—A forty-day Lenten period preceding Christmas—
November 15-December 25 (November 28-January 7)

*PRESENTATION TO THE TEMPLE OF
THE VIRGIN MARY .... November 21 (December 4)

Dates shown first denote Julian calendar date—Dates
in parentheses denote Gregorian calendar date.

**Greatest Festival of the Eastern Orthodox Church year.

*One of the Twelve Most Important Orthodox Feast Days.

Every Wednesday and Friday of the year—with specified exceptions—
are fast days.

RELIGIOUS DEDICATIONS OF THE DAYS OF THE WEEK

Monday is dedicated to the Angels.
Tuesday is dedicated to John the Baptist and the prophets.
Wednesday is dedicated to the Betrayal of Jesus.
Thursday is dedicated to the Apostles and St. Nicholas.
Friday is dedicated to the Crucifixion and Burial of Christ.
Saturday is dedicated to the Martyrs and our departed ones.
Sunday is dedicated to the Resurrection.

DAILY CYCLE OF SERVICES

In the Eastern Orthodox Church the day is reckoned from sunset to sunset, not from midnight to midnight.

The Orthodox Church day, with the services traditionally ascribed to the various times is as follows:

Period	Time	Service
	DAYTIME	
First Hour	6 A.M. to 9 A.M.	First Hour
Third Hour	9 A.M. to Noon	Third Hour
Sixth Hour	12 Noon to 3 P.M.	Sixth Hour
Ninth Hour	3 P.M. to 6 P.M.	Ninth Hour
	NIGHT	
Evening	6 P.M. to 9 P.M.	Vespers
Midnight	9 P.M. to 12 P.M.	Aftervespers
Cockcrow	12 Midnight to 3 A.M.	Mesonyktics
Morning	3 A.M. to 6 A.M.	Orthos

THE HOURS

The simplest form of Eastern Orthodox service is the Hours, performed during the different hours of the day.

First Hour (7 A.M.) Beginning of the Day
Third Hour (9 A.M.) Holy Spirit descended on the Apostles
Sixth Hour (Noon) Christ was nailed to the Cross
Ninth Hour (3 P.M.) Christ gave up His Spirit, dying on the Cross
    Before the Liturgy, the Third and Sixth Hours are recited
    Before Vespers, the Ninth Hour is read

DATES OF THE GREAT LENT AND EASTER SEASON
1968 TO 1973
(All dates shown as they occur on the modern Gregorian Calendar)

	1968*	1969	1970	1971	1972*	1973
PRE-LENT						
1st Sunday—						
SUNDAY OF PUBLICAN AND PHARISEE	Feb. 11	Feb. 2	Feb. 15	Feb. 7	Jan. 30	Feb. 18
2nd Sunday—						
SUNDAY OF THE PRODIGAL SON	Feb. 18	Feb. 9	Feb. 22	Feb. 14	Feb. 6	Feb. 25
3rd Sunday—						
MEAT FARE SUNDAY	Feb. 25	Feb. 16	Mar. 1	Feb. 21	Feb. 13	Mar. 4
4th Sunday—						
CHEESE FARE SUNDAY	Mar. 3	Feb. 23	Mar. 8	Feb. 28	Feb. 20	Mar. 11
THE GREAT LENT						
Beginning of Lent, Seven Weeks before Easter	Mar. 4	Feb. 24	Mar. 9	Mar. 1	Feb. 21	Mar. 12
1st Sunday of Lent—						
ORTHODOX SUNDAY	Mar. 10	Mar. 2	Mar. 15	Mar. 7	Feb. 27	Mar. 18
2nd Sunday of Lent—	Mar. 17	Mar. 9	Mar. 22	Mar. 14	Mar. 5	Mar. 25
3rd Sunday of Lent—						
ADORATION OF THE CROSS	Mar. 24	Mar. 16	Mar. 29	Mar. 21	Mar. 12	April 1
4th Sunday of Lent—	Mar. 31	Mar. 23	April 5	Mar. 28	Mar. 19	April 8
5th Sunday of Lent—						
BLACK SUNDAY	April 7	Mar. 30	April 12	April 4	Mar. 26	April 15
LAZARUS SATURDAY	April 13	April 5	April 18	April 10	April 1	April 21
6th Sunday of Lent—						
PALM OR WILLOW SUNDAY	April 14	April 6	April 19	April 11	April 2	April 22
HOLY WEEK or PASSION WEEK						
Holy or Maundy Thursday LAST SUPPER	April 18	April 10	April 23	April 15	April 6	April 26
GREAT FRIDAY or GOOD FRIDAY	April 19	April 11	April 24	April 16	April 7	April 27
EASTER SUNDAY FEAST OF FEASTS	April 21	April 13	April 26	April 18	April 9	April 29
LORD'S ASCENSION— Forty Days after Easter	May 30	May 22	June 4	May 27	May 18	June 7
PENTECOST—Descent of the Holy Spirit—50th Day after Easter	June 9	June 1	June 14	June 6	May 28	June 17
ST. PETER & PAUL'S LENT BEGINS	June 17	June 9	June 22	June 14	June 5	June 25

EASTER SEASON DATES AS OBSERVED BY OTHER THAN ORTHODOX CHURCHES

	1968*	1969	1970	1971	1972*	1973
LENT BEGINS	Feb. 28	Feb. 19	Feb. 11	Feb. 24	Feb. 16	Mar. 7
PALM SUNDAY	April 7	Mar. 30	Mar. 22	April 4	Mar. 26	April 15
GOOD FRIDAY	April 12	April 4	Mar. 27	April 7	Mar. 31	April 20
EASTER SUNDAY	April 14	April 6	Mar. 29	April 11	April 2	April 22
ASCENSION	May 23	May 15	May 7	May 20	May 11	May 31
PENTECOST	June 2	May 25	May 17	May 30	May 21	June 10

* Leap Year

EPISTLE AND GOSPEL TEXTS FOR THE ORTHODOX YEAR

Sunday	*Epistle*	*Gospel*
Sunday of the Publican and Pharisee....	II Tim. 3:10-15	Luke 18:10-14
Sunday of the Prodigal Son.............	I Cor. 6:12-20	Luke 15:11-32
Meat Fast Sunday	I Cor. 8:8-9:2	Matt. 25:31-46
Cheese Fast Sunday	Rom. 13:11-14:1	Matt. 6:14-21
First Sunday of Lent	Heb. 11:24-26; 11:32-12:2	John 1:43-51
Second Sunday of Lent.................	Heb. 1:10-23; 7:26-8:2	Mark 2:1-12
		John 10:9-16
Third Sunday of Lent	Heb. 4:14-5:6	Mark 8:34-9:1
Fourth Sunday of Lent	Heb. 6:13-20; Eph. 5:9-16	Mark 9:17-31
		Matt. 4:25-5:12
Fifth Sunday of Lent	Heb. 9:11-14	Mark 10:32-45
	Gal. 3:23-29	Luke 7:36-50
Palm Sunday	Phil. 4:4-9	John 12:1-8
Easter Sunday–Divine Liturgy	Acts 1:1-8	John 1:1-17
Vesper Service		John 20:19-25
Sunday of St. Thomas	Acts 5:12-20	John 20:19-31
Sunday of the Myrrh-Bearing Women..	Acts 6:1-7	Mark 15:43-16:8
Sunday of the Paralytic	Acts 9:32-42	John 5:1-15
Sunday of the Samaritan Woman	Acts 11:19-26; 29-30	John 4:5-42
Sunday of the Blind Man	Acts 16:16-34	John 9:1-38
Sunday of the Holy Fathers	Acts 20:16-18; 26-36	John 17:1-13
Holy Pentecost Sunday	Acts 2:1-11	John 7:37-52
		John 8:12
First Sunday after Pentecost	Heb. 11:33-12:2	Matt. 10:32-33
		Matt. 10:37-38
Second Sunday after Pentecost	Rom. 2:10-16	Matt. 4:18-23
Third Sunday after Pentecost	Rom. 5:1-10	Matt. 6:22-33
Fourth Sunday after Pentecost	Rom. 6:18-23	Matt. 8:5-13
Fifth Sunday after Pentecost	Rom. 10:1-10	Matt. 8:28-9:1
Sixth Sunday after Pentecost	Rom. 12:6-14	Matt. 9:1-8
Seventh Sunday after Pentecost	Rom. 15:1-7	Matt. 9:27-35
Eighth Sunday after Pentecost	I Cor. 1:10-17	**Matt. 14:14-22**
Ninth Sunday after Pentecost	I Cor. 3:9-17	Matt. 14:22-34
Tenth Sunday after Pentecost	I Cor. 4:9-16	Matt. 17:14-23
Eleventh Sunday after Pentecost	I Cor. 9:2-12	Matt. 18:23-35
Twelfth Sunday after Pentecost	I Cor. 15:1-11	Matt. 19:16-26
Thirteenth Sunday after Pentecost	I Cor. 16:13-24	Matt. 21:33-42
Fourteenth Sunday after Pentecost	II Cor. 1:21-2:4	Matt. 22:2-14
Fifteenth Sunday after Pentecost	II Cor. 4:6-15	Matt. 22:35-46
Sixteenth Sunday after Pentecost	II Cor. 6:1-10	Matt. 25:14-30
		Luke 8:8
Seventeenth Sunday after Pentecost	II Cor. 6:16-17:1	Matt. 15:21-28
Eighteenth Sunday after Pentecost	II Cor. 9:6-11	Luke 5:1-11
Nineteenth Sunday after Pentecost	II Cor. 11:31-12:9	Luke 6:31-36
Twentieth Sunday after Pentecost	Gal. 1:11-19	Luke 7:11-16
Twenty-first Sunday after Pentecost	Gal. 2:16-20	Luke 8:5-15
Twenty-second Sunday after Pentecost .	Gal. 6:11-18	Luke 16:19-31
Twenty-third Sunday after Pentecost ...	Eph. 2:4-10	Luke 8:27-39
Twenty-fourth Sunday after Pentecost ..	Eph. 2:14-22	Luke 8:41-56
Twenty-fifth Sunday after Pentecost ...	Eph. 4:1-7	Luke 10:25-37
Twenty-sixth Sunday after Pentecost ...	Eph. 5:8-19	Luke 12:16-21
Twenty-seventh Sunday after Pentecost.	Eph. 6:10-17	Luke 13:10-17
Twenty-eighth Sunday after Pentecost ..	Col. 1:12-18	Luke 14:16-24
Twenty-ninth Sunday after Pentecost ..	Col. 3:4-11	Luke 17:12-19
Thirtieth Sunday after Pentecost	Col. 3:12-16	Luke 18:18-27
Thirty-first Sunday after Pentecost	I Tim. 1:15-17	Luke 18:35-43
Thirty-second Sunday after Pentecost ..	I Tim. 4:9-15	Luke 19:1-10
Sunday before Exaltation of Cross	Gal. 6:11-18	John 3:13-17

Sunday	Epistle	Gospel
Sunday after Exaltation of Cross	Gal. 2:16–20	Mark 8:34–38; 9:1
Sunday before Christmas	Heb. 11:9–10; 17:40	Matt. 1:1–25
Sunday after Christmas	Gal. 1:11–19	Matt. 2:13–23
Sunday before Epiphany	II Tim. 4:5–8	Mark 1:1–8
Sunday after Epiphany	Eph. 4:7–13	Matt. 4:12–17

SCRIPTURE READINGS FOR MAJOR HOLY DAYS

Nativity of the Virgin Mary	Phil. 2:5–11	Luke 10:38–42; 11:27–28
Elevation of the Cross of Our Lord ...	I Cor. 1:18–24	John 19:6–11, 13–20, 25–28, 30–35
Presentation of the Virgin Mary........	Heb. 9:1–7	Luke 10:38–42; 11:27–28
Nativity of Our Lord (Christmas Day)..	Gal. 4:4–7	Matt. 2:1–12
Epiphany—Baptism of Our Lord........	Tit. 2:11–14; 3:4–7	Matt. 3:13–17
Presentation of Our Lord in the Temple.	Heb. 7:7–11	Luke 2:22–40
Annunciation of the Virgin Mary.......	Heb. 2:11–18	Luke 1:24–38
Transfiguration of Our Lord	II Peter 1:10–19	Matt. 17:1–9
Assumption of the Virgin Mary........	Philip. 2:5–11	Luke 10:38–42; 11:27–28
Entry of Our Lord into Jerusalem	Philip. 4:4–9	John 12:1–18
Ascension of Our Lord	Acts 1:1–12	Luke 24:36–53
Pentecost—Descent of the Holy Spirit...	Acts 2:1–11	Luke 16:15–18; 17:1–4
Feast of the Holy Spirit................	Eph. 5:9–19	Matt. 18:10–20

SUNDAY MATINS GOSPEL READINGS

1. Matt. 28:16–20
2. Mark 16:1–8
3. Mark 16:9–20
4. Luke 24:1–12
5. Luke 24:12–35
6. Luke 24:36–53
7. John 20:1–10
8. John 20:11–18
9. John 20:19–31
10. John 21:1–14
11. John 21:15–25

12 GOSPELS ON THE PASSION OF OUR LORD ON HOLY THURSDAY

1. John 13:31–18:1
2. John 18:1–28
3. Matt. 26:57–75
4. John 18:28–19:16
5. Matt. 27:3–32
6. Mark 15:16–32
7. Matt. 27:34–54
8. Luke 23:32–49
9. John 19:25–37
10. Mark 15:43–47
11. John 19:38–42
12. Matt. 27:62–66

Transfiguration Hill in Palestine

DEDICATED DAYS OF THE ORTHODOX YEAR
DAY COMMEMORATED

Date Observed on the Julian Calendar		Date Observed on the Gregorian Calendar
January 1	The Circumcision of Jesus Christ	January 14
January 1	St. Basil the Great—(also one of the Three Hierarchs commemorated on January 30th)	January 14
January 3	Malachi the Prophet Three Saints	January 16
January 6	Epiphany or Theophany—Baptism of Jesus Great Blessing of Waters	January 19
January 7	The Solemn Memorial of St. John the Baptist (He is also commemorated on June 24, August 29 and September 23)	January 20
January 10	St. Gregory of Nyssa	January 23
January 17	St. Anthony the Great	January 30
January 18	St. Athanasius and St. Cyril of Alexandria (St. Cyril is also commemorated on June 9)	January 31
January 19	St. Macarius	February 1
January 20	St. Euthymius	February 2
January 21	St. Maximus the Confessor (Also commemorated on August 12)	February 3
January 22	St. Timothy the Apostle	February 4
January 25	St. Gregory the Theologian	February 7
January 27	St. John Chrysostom (He is also commemorated on November 13 and January 30)	February 9
January 28	St. Ephraem the Syrian	February 10
January 30	The Three Hierarchs—Basil the Great, Gregory the Theologian and John Chrysostom. (St. Basil also commemorated on January 1, St. Gregory on January 25 and St. John Chrysostom on January 27 and November 13)	February 12
January 31	St. Cyrus the Unmercenary and St. John the Unmercenary	February 13
February 2	Presentation of Jesus in the Temple Purification—Blessing of Candles	February 15
February 3	St. Anna the Prophetess and St. Simeon the God-Receiver	February 16
February 5	St. Agatha the Martyr	February 18
February 6	St. Julian, the Martyr of Homs	February 19
February 10	St. Charalampos	February 23
February 12	St. Meletius of Antioch	February 25
February 17	St. Theodore of Tyre	March 2 (March 1st on Leap Years)
February 18	St. Leo	March 3 (March 2nd on Leap Years)
February 21	St. Eustathius of Antioch	March 6 (March 5th on Leap Years)
February 23	St. Polycarp of Smyrna	March 8 (March 7th on Leap Years)
February 26	St. Porphyrius of Gaza	March 11 (March 10th on Leap Years)
March 1	St. Eudoxia	March 14
March 4	St. Gerasimos	March 17
March 9	The Forty Martyrs of Sebaste	March 22
March 11	St. Sophronius of Jerusalem	March 24
March 13	St. Nicephorus of Constantinople (Also commemorated on June 2)	March 26

Date Observed on the Julian Calendar		Date Observed on the Gregorian Calendar
March 14	St. Benedict	March 27
March 18	St. Cyril of Jerusalem	March 31
March 25	The Annunciation of the Virgin Mary (She is also commemorated on August 15, September 8, and November 21)	April 7
March 26	Archangel Gabriel (Also commemorated on July 13 and November 8)	April 8
March 30	St. John Climakos—Author of "The Ladder" (Also commemorated on 4th Sunday of Lent)	April 12
April 1	St. Mary of Egypt	April 14
April 2	St. Titus	April 15
April 13	St. Martin	April 26
April 15	St. Crescens	April 28
April 23	St. George, the Victorious Great Martyr	May 6
April 25	St. Mark the Evangelist	May 8
April 30	St. James the Apostle, Son of Zebedee	May 13
May 1	St. Jeremiah the Prophet	May 14
May 2	St. Athanasius (Also commemorated on January 18)	May 15
May 5	St. Irene	May 18
May 8	St. John the Evangelist (Also commemorated on September 26)	May 21
May 9	St. Christopher Isaac the Prophet	May 22
May 10	St. Simon the Zealot	May 23
May 12	St. Germanos of Constantinople	May 25
May 15	St. Pachomius	May 28
May 17	St. June	May 30
May 21	St. Constantine and St. Helena	June 3
May 29	St. Theodosia	June 11
June 2	St. Nicephorus of Constantinople (Also commemorated on March 13)	June 15
June 5	St. Dorotheus	June 18
June 6	St. Marcia	June 19
June 9	St. Cyril of Alexandria (Also commemorated on January 18)	June 22
June 11	The Apostles Bartholomew and Barnabas	June 24
June 17	St. Manuel	June 30
June 18	St. Leontius	July 1
June 19	St. Jude	July 2
June 24	Nativity of St. John the Baptist (John the Forerunner is also commemorated on January 7, August 29 and September 23)	July 7
June 24	St. Elizabeth (Also commemorated on September 5)	July 7
June 24	St. Zacharias (Also commemorated on September 5th and September 23)	July 7
June 29	The Holy Apostles Peter and Paul	July 12
June 30	Feast of the Twelve Apostles	July 13
July 1	St. Cosmas and St. Damian (They are also commemorated on November 1st)	July 14
July 3	St. Hyacinth	July 16
July 4	St. Andrew of Crete	July 17
July 5	St. Agnes	July 18
July 11	St. Olga, Princess of Kiev	July 24
July 11	St. Euphemia (Also commemorated on September 16)	July 24
July 13–19	The Holy Fathers of the First Six Ecumenical Councils (On the Sunday falling between the 13th and 19th of July)	July 26–August 1

Date Observed on the Julian Calendar		Date Observed on the Gregorian Calendar
July 17	St. Marina	July 30
July 19	St. Macrina	August 1
July 20	St. Elias the Prophet	August 2
July 22	St. Mary Magdalene	August 4
July 24	St. Christina	August 6
July 25	St. Anne (Also commemorated on September 9 and December 9)	August 7
July 26	St. Paraskeve	August 8
July 27	St. Panteleimon	August 9
August 6	Transfiguration of Christ	August 19
August 8	St. Aemilian	August 21
August 9	St. Matthias	August 22
August 10	St. Lawrence	August 23
August 12	St. Maximus the Confessor (Also commemorated on January 21)	August 25
August 15	Assumption (Falling Asleep) of the Virgin Mary (She is also commemorated on March 25, September 8 and November 21)	August 28
August 18	St. Florus	August 31
August 20	Samuel the Prophet	September 2
August 21	St. Thaddeus	September 3
August 26	St. Natalie	September 8
August 29	St. John the Baptist (Also commemorated on January 7, June 24 and September 23)	September 11
August 30	St. Alexander of Constantinople	September 12
September 1	Byzantine Church Year which is followed by churches of the Eastern Orthodox faith begins	September 14
September 1	St. Simeon Stylites of Antioch	September 14
September 4	Moses the Prophet	September 17
September 5	St. Elizabeth and St. Zacharias (Also commemorated on June 24)	September 18
September 6	St. Michael (Also commemorated on November 8)	September 19
September 8	Nativity of the Virgin Mary (She is also commemorated on March 25, August 15 and November 21)	September 21
September 9	St. Anna and St. Joachim (Anna is also commemorated on July 25 and December 9)	September 22
September 11	St. Theodora of Alexandria	September 24
September 14	Elevation of the Precious and Life-Giving Cross	September 27
September 16	St. Euphemia (Also commemorated on July 11)	September 29
September 17	Faith, Hope and Charity St. Sophia	September 30
September 18	St. Ariadne	October 1
September 23	St. John the Baptist (He is also commemorated on January 7, June 24 and August 29)	October 6
September 23	St. Zacharias (Also commemorated on September 5th and June 24)	October 6
September 24	St. Thecla	October 7
September 25	St. Euphrosyne	October 8
September 26	St. John the Evangelist (Also commemorated on May 8)	October 9
September 30	St. Gregory the Illuminator	October 13
October 1	Protection of the Virgin Mary	October 14
October 1	St. Romanus Melodos St. Ananias	October 14
October 2	St. Cyprian	October 15
October 3	St. Dionysius and St. Thomas	October 16
October 6	St. Thomas the Apostle	October 19

Date Observed on the Julian Calendar		Date Observed on the Gregorian Calendar
October 7	St. Bacchus and St. Sergius	October 20
October 8	St. Pelagia	October 21
October 9	St. James, son of Alpheus	October 22
October 11-17	The Holy Fathers of the Seventh Ecumenical Council (Observed the Sunday falling between the 11th and 17th of October)	October 24-30
October 18	St. Luke the Evangelist	October 31
October 23	St. James the Apostle	November 5
October 24	St. Arethas	November 6
October 26	St. Demetrius	November 8
October 27	St. Nestor	November 9
October 28	St. Terence	November 10
October 31	St. Narcissus	November 13
November 1	St. Cosmas and St. Damian	November 14
November 8	The Archangels Michael, Gabriel and Raphael and all the bodiless Powers (Gabriel is also commemorated on March 26 and July 13; Michael is also commemorated on September 6)	November 21
November 11	St. Victor and St. Theodore Studites	November 24
November 13	St. John Chrysostom (He is also commemorated on January 27 and January 30)	November 26
November 14	St. Philip the Apostle	November 27
November 15	Beginning of the Fast of the Nativity	November 28
November 16	St. Matthew the Apostle	November 29
November 17	St. Gregory the Wonderworker	November 30
November 21	The Presentation of the Virgin Mary (She is also commemorated on March 25, August 15 and September 8)	December 4
November 25	St. Catherine of Sinai	December 8
November 29	St. Philomena	December 12
November 30	St. Andrew, the First Called Apostle	December 13
December 1	St. Nahum the Prophet	December 14
December 4	St. Barbara and St. John of Damascus	December 17
December 5	St. Sabbas	December 18
December 6	St. Nicholas the Wonderworker	December 19
December 9	St. Anna (She is also commemorated on July 25 and September 9)	December 22
December 12	St. Spiridon	December 25
December 13	St. Lucy	December 26
Dec. 11-17	The Sunday of the Holy Forefathers (Observed on the Sunday falling between December 11 and December 17)	December 24-30
December 17	St. Daniel the Prophet	December 30
Dec. 18-24	The Sunday of the Genealogy (Observed on the Sunday falling between December 18 and December 24)	December 31-January 6
December 20	St. Ignatius of Antioch	January 2
December 21	St. Juliana	January 3
December 22	St. Anastasia	January 4
December 24	St. Eugenia	January 6
December 25	The Nativity of Jesus—Christmas	January 7
December 26	Memorial of the Virgin Mary	January 8
December 26-January 1	Sunday after Christmas (Commemorates St. Joseph, David the Prophet and St. James. Observed the Sunday falling between December 26 and January 1)	January 8-14
December 27	St. Stephen—the First Martyr	January 9
December 30	St. Anysia	January 12
December 31	St. Melania	January 13

10

Orthodox Dictionary

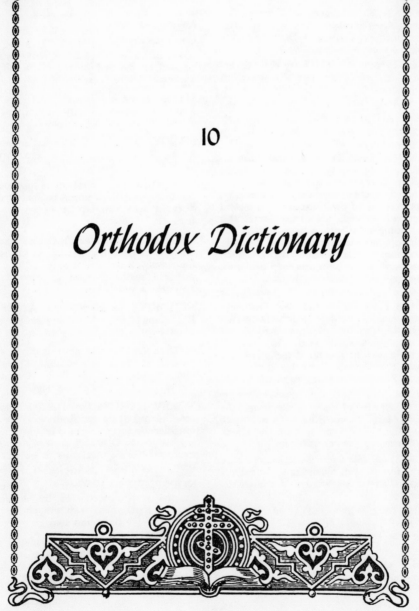

A DICTIONARY OF THE EASTERN ORTHODOX CHURCH

Names and words with their pronunciations and application to the Orthodox faith.

A

ABBOT (ăb'ŭt)—The head of a monastery of monks.

ABSOLUTION (ăb'sŏ lū'shŭn)—The declaration of God's forgiveness of sins pronounced by the priest after the confession of sins in the Sacrament of Penance (Confession).

ABSTINENCE (ăb'stĭ nĕns)—Self-denial. Refraining from gratification of appetite. Days of abstinence are the Fast Days when the eating of meat is not permitted.

ADVENT (ăd'vent)—The forty day fast before Christmas beginning November 28, new calendar.

AER (âr)—A large veil used to cover the chalice and paten during the Divine Liturgy. Usually made of the same material as the priest's vestments.

AFFINITY (ă fĭn'ĭ tĭ)—A spiritual relationship becoming an impediment to marriage. Godparents contract a spiritual affinity with the child through Baptism. In Matrimony, blood relatives of the husband to the second degree of kindred, inclusive, contract this relationship of affinity with the wife. The same applies to blood relatives of the wife in relation to the husband. Between such relatives, dispensation is necessary to permit marriage.

AGNETS (ag'nĕts)—The sacrificial lamb of the Old Testament. In the New Testament Jesus was symbolically called the Lamb; accordingly, Orthodox churches attribute the name Agnets to Christ in the Sacrament of Eucharist and the portion of the holy bread taken from the prosphora for the mystic transubstantiation is called Agnets.

AKATHIST (ăk'ă thĭst)—A service consisting of many hymns of praise to the Savior, the Virgin Mary or some Saint, sung in church or at home. The word is from the Greek word meaning "not to sit."

ALB (ălb)—A full-length vestment reaching to the feet is worn by the priest under the chasuble during celebration of the Divine Liturgy.

ALLELUIA (ăl'ĕ lōō'yà)—Derived from the Hebrew, meaning "Praise the Lord." It is sung after the reading of the Epistle at the Liturgy and at the end of the Psalms.

ALPHA and **OMEGA** (ăl'fà) (ō mē'gà)—First and last letters of the Greek alphabet; symbolize the beginning and the end.

ALTAR (ôl'tĕr)—Derived from the Latin, meaning "a place of sacrifice." In the Eastern Church it is the elevated area (Sanctuary) separated from the nave by the Iconostas. The Prestol upon which the sacrifice of the Eucharist is brought is located here.

ALTAR BREAD (ôl'tĕr) (brĕd)—Round loaves of bread made from pure wheat flour, used in the Divine Liturgy. Also known as Prosphora.

AMEN (ā"mĕn') or (à'mĕn)—From the Hebrew, meaning "so be it"; a response sung or said at the end of prayers, signifying approval of what has preceded.

AMVON (ăm'vŏn)—The elevated area, also known as Ambo, directly in front of the Royal Doors, used as the pulpit.

ANALOY (ăn'à loi)—A high table, usually having a sloped top which is used as a Gospel stand or an icon stand.

ANAPHORA (ă năf'ŏ rā)—The portion of the Liturgy of the Faithful beginning with, "Let us stand aright, let us stand with fear. . . ."

ANATHEMA (à năth'ê mà)—Solemn excommunication from the Church. In Orthodox Cathedrals on the first Sunday of the Great lent the anathema upon all heretics and apostates is proclaimed.

ANCHORITE (ăn'kō rīte) also **ANCHORET** (ăng'kō rĕt)—A hermit confined to a solitary cell.

ANGEL (ān'jĕl)—A pure bodiless spirit created by God before man. There are nine degrees of angels. Each Monday of the year is dedicated to the angels.

ANDREW'S CROSS (krôs)—an "X" shaped cross named from St. Andrew as he was crucified on such a cross. The lower slanting bar on the Orthodox cross is sometimes interpreted as St. Andrew's as he was the first to preach the Gospel to the Slavs.

ANOINTMENT (à noynt'mĕnt)—Anointing the sick with oil is one of the Sacraments and is accompanied with prayers for the healing of the body and soul.

ANNUNCIATION (ă nŭn"sĭ ā'shŭn—Feast celebrated in commemoration of the visit of the Archangel Gabriel to the Virgin Mary to announce to her that she was to be the Mother of the Son of God.

ANTICHRIST (ăn'tĭ Krīst)—The great personal opponent of Christ who is to appear before the end of the world and who will be overthrown by Christ at His second coming.

ANTIDOR (ăn'tĭ dōr)—The name given to the pieces of holy bread from the prosphora which are distributed to worshipers after the Divine Liturgy. From the Greek, it means "instead of a reward."

ANTIMINS (ăn'tĭ mĭns)—Also known as Corporal, an antimins is a silk cloth with a sketch of the entombment of Christ inscribed on it and a part of a relic sewed into it. A combined Greek-Latin word meaning "in place of a table," the antimins is absolutely necessary in the celebration of the Divine Liturgy.

ANTIPHON (ăn'tĭ fŏn)—Verses from the Psalms, each followed by anthems, sung on Great Holy Days at the Divine Liturgy after each of the first three litanies.

APOCALYPSE (á pŏk'á lĭps)—Prophetic New Testament book written by the Apostle John. The final book of the Bible, also known as Revelations.

APOCRYPHA (á pŏk'rĭ fá)—Certain Old Testament books not considered Canonical but included in Orthodox and Roman Catholic Bibles.

APOSTLE (á pos'l)—From the Greek, meaning "one who is sent." The name given by Christ to the Twelve Disciples. The Orthodox Church applies this name also to the Seventy Disciples of Christ who preached the Gospel. Some outstanding Christian workers have also become known as Equal-to-the-Apostles.

ARCHBISHOP (ärch'bĭsh'ŭp)—Chief of the bishops in a church province.

ARCHDEACON (ärch'dē'kn)—The chief deacon. If married, the title is protodeacon. The Martyr Stephen was the first archdeacon.

ARCHIMANDRITE (är"kĭ măn'drīt)—A monastic rank next below the bishop in the church hierarchy. From the Greek, meaning "the head of a monastery."

ARCHPRIEST (ärch'prēst)—Priest honored with special dignity or assigned special duties.

ARTOS (är'tŏs)—Easter bread representing the Bread of Eternal Life. The Artos is kept on the lectern during Easter week and is broken up and given to the worshipers the eighth day after Easter.

ASCENSION DAY (á sĕn'shŭn Dāy)—Movable feast day observed forty days after Easter to commemorate the Ascension of Christ into Heaven.

ASSUMPTION (á sŭmp'shŭn)—Feast day celebrating the falling asleep of the Virgin Mary.

ASTERISK (ăs'tēr ĭsk)—The asterisk, also called the star, is a sacred vessel placed over the paten to keep the holy bread and particles disposed around it in a prescribed order. Also serves to support the aer and veil covering the chalice and paten.

B

BANNER (băn'ĕr)—Metallic or brocade cloth inscribed with sacred icons, carried at the head of processionals on long poles.

BANNS (bănz)—Proclamation announced in church of an intended marriage. Banns are repeated three times.

BAPTISM (băp'tizm)—Sacrament washing away original sin and joins person baptized to the church. Baptism, usually performed by a priest, may be administered by a layman in cases of emergency.

BEATITUDES (bē ăt'ĭ tūdz)—The nine blessings given by Christ in His Sermon on the Mount. They are sung at the time of the Little Entrance in the Divine Liturgy.

BELFRY (bĕl'frĭ)—Part of the church where the church bells are hung, usually a tower above the front of the church.

BELLS (bĕls)—Used to summon the faithful to worship. They are rung at certain progressive points in the service, while the Holy Gifts are being consecrated, during processionals and are tolled in mourning for the dead.

BENEDICTION (bĕn"ĕ dĭk'shŭn)—Blessing given by the priest at the conclusion of the Divine Liturgy.

BETROTHAL (bê trŏth'ăl) or (bê trŏth'ăl)—First part of the Marriage ceremony in which a formal and binding promise is made and rings are placed on the fingers of the bride and groom.

BIBLE (bī'bl)—Sacred Books including the Old and New Testaments. Holy Writings of men inspired by God.

BISHOP (bĭsh'ŭp)—One of the chief orders of Orthodox clergy, endowed with the right of laying on of hands to ordain priests and deacons. A bishop is usually in charge of a diocese.

BOWING (bou'ĭng)—Attitude of the body in Divine Worship to express reverence.

BYZANTINE (bĭ zăn'tĭn)—Style of architecture popular with Orthodox churches, developed in Byzantium, now called Istanbul.

C

CALENDAR (kăl'ĕn dȧr)—Orderly arrangement of the days, weeks and months of the year. The Orthodox Church uses the old Julian calendar in reckoning church days.

CALVARY (kăl'vȧ rĭ)—Golgotha, the Mount where Christ was crucified.

CANDELABRUM (kăn''dĕ lā'brŭm)—Large, branched candlestick, usually designed for seven candles to symbolize the seven sacraments, the seven great Orthodox holidays connected with Christ, the seven Ecumenical Councils, and the seven days of creation.

CANDLES (kăn'dls)—Used profusely in Orthodox churches to express the warmth of devotion and as symbols of the light of Christ.

CANON (kăn'ŭn)—From the Greek, meaning rule. Applies to a rule given by a priest to a worshiper after confession for spiritual healing and strength and is also applied to the collection of hymns sung at Matins.

CANON LAW (kăn'ŭn lô)—Rules or laws relating to faith, morals and discipline as prescribed by the Ecumenical and Provincial Councils and the Holy Fathers.

CANONIZATION (kăn''ŭn ī zā'shun)—Proclamation by church authorities on the sanctity and glory of a faithful departed. Through this public testimony the person canonized is inscribed in the list of Saints.

CANON OF SCRIPTURE (kăn'ŭn skrĭp'tŭr)—The list of inspired books accepted on church authority as the Word of God—the Bible.

CASSOCK (kăs'ŭk)—A long black garment, the ordinary dress of priests. Although they are usually black, blue, purple and maroon are also common.

CATECHISM (kăt'ê kizm)—Elementary Christian doctrine instruction in question and answer form.

CATHEDRA (kȧ thē'drȧ)—Bishop's throne in back of the Altar. The Amvon is also sometimes given this name.

CATHEDRAL (kȧ thē'drăl)—Main church of a Diocese where the bishop has his throne.

CAROL (kăr'ŭl)—A joyous, festive hymn, simple in tune, sung at Christmas.

CATECHUMEN (kăt''ê kū'men)—A person preparing for Baptism. In former times, catechumens were permitted to remain in church for only the first two portions of the Divine Liturgy.

CATHOLIC (kăth'ŏ lĭk)—In literal meaning, denotes universal or all-embracing. Signifies that the Church of Christ is for all ages, for all nations, for all races and is the Ark of Salvation for all mankind.

CELEBRATION (sĕl'ê brā'shun)—Sacred performance of the Divine Liturgy and specifically, the Holy Communion.

CELEBRANT (sĕl'ê brănt)—Person performing Holy Communion—a bishop or priest. A deacon may not celebrate the Holy Eucharist but may assist.

CELIBACY—(sĕl'ĭ bȧ sĭ) or (sê lĭb'ȧ sĭ)—In the Roman Church, a rule forbidding marriage in the clergy. In the Orthodox Church, those entering the priesthood cannot marry after being ordained. Orthodox bishops are chosen from celibates or widowers who have taken monastic vows.

CENSER (sĕn'sêr)—Vessel used for burning incense in church ceremonies.

CENSOR (sĕn'sŏr) or (sĕn'sêr)—Theologian appointed to examine books for ecclesiastical approval prior to publication. The censor ascertains that publications contain nothing contrary to the Orthodox doctrine.

CHALICE (chăl'ĭs)—A sacred vessel, in the form of a cup, made of precious metal and consecrated to contain the wine which becomes the Blood of Christ during the Divine Liturgy.

CHANCEL (chȧn'sĕl)—The area around the altar, also called the Sanctuary, separated from the body of the church by the Iconostas.

CHAPEL (chăp'ĕl)—A small house of worship where there is no parish.

CHAPLAIN (chăp'lĭn)—A priest in the armed services or authorized to officiate in military chapels. Also denotes a priest ministering to the religious needs of a school, fraternity, or public institution.

CHAPTER (chăp'têr)—A division of a book of the Bible.

CHASUBLE (chăz'ủ bl)—A large garment without sleeves, also called a Felon, short in front and with an opening for the head which is worn as the principal vestment by a priest in celebrating the Divine Liturgy.

CHRISM (krĭzm)—Holy Oil, also called Myrrh, used in the Sacrament of Chrismation. Chrism is mixed and blessed by a group of bishops on Thursday of Holy Week.

CHRISMATION (krĭz mā'shun)—Also called Confirmation, is the Sacrament by which believers receive the Holy Spirit. In the Orthodox Church, it is administered immediately after Baptism.

CHRISTEN (krĭs'n)—To name an infant at Baptism; to receive into the Church by Baptism. Baptism is often called Christening.

CHRISTIAN (krĭs'chăn)—One baptized into the Church to become a follower of Christ. Followers of Christ were first called Christians at Antioch.

CHRISTIAN NAME (krĭs'chăn nām)—The name given and received in the Sacrament of Baptism.

CHRISTMAS (krĭs'màs)—The Feast of the Nativity or the Birthday of our Lord. Observed on December 25, old calendar, which is January 7th on the new Gregorian calendar.

CHURCH (chûrch)—A divinely instituted community of believers. Members of the Orthodox Church are united by the Orthodox faith, the laws of God, the hierarchy and the Sacraments.

CHURCH MILITANT (chûrch mĭl'ĭ tănt)—Members of the church on earth in warfare against sin and evil as distinguished from the Church Triumphant in Heaven.

CHURCHING OF WOMEN (chûrch ing)—The blessing of women after childbirth. In the life of a Christian mother corresponds to the Feast of Purification of the Virgin Mary.

CLERGY (klûr'jĭ)—Those ordained to the threefold ministry of the Church—bishops, priests and deacons, as distinguished from laymen.

COMMUNION, HOLY (kŏ mūn'yŭn)—The Sacrament of Holy Eucharist. After proper confession and absolution, the worshiper receives sanctifying grace through the true Body and Blood of Christ. Those who are to receive Communion must fast from midnight previous to the hour of receiving this sacrament.

COMMUNION OF SAINTS (kŏ mūn'yŭn sāntz)—All members of the Church, in heaven and on earth are in communion with each other, as being one Body in Christ.

COMPLINE, GRAND (kŏm'plīn, grănd)—A service of worship said after nightfall in monasteries. In church parishes it is combined with Matins to form the All-Night Vigil Service.

CONFESSION (kŏn fĕsh'ŭn)—Acknowledgement of sin before God in the presence of a priest; the Sacrament of Penance.

CONFESSOR (kŏn fes'ĕr)—Person who hears confession or one who has suffered persecution for his faith.

CONFIRMATION (kŏn''fĕr mā'shŭn)—The Sacrament of Chrismation.

CONSECRATION (kŏn''sĕ krā'shŭn)—The dedication of anything to Divine Service or elevation of a member of the clergy to the rank of bishop.

CONVENT (kŏn'vĕnt)—The dwelling of religious women living under monastic rules.

CORPORAL (kôr'pŏ răl)—The cloth on the Altar on which the Holy Eucharist is consecrated. Also called Antimins.

CREED (krēd)—Articles of faith formulated by the Ecumenical Councils (Nicene Creed) or by the Holy Fathers (Athanasian Creed).

CROSIER (krō'zhĕr)—Staff carried by a bishop as a symbol of authority by which he rules his flock.

CROSS, ORTHODOX (krôs, ôr'thŏ dŏks)—The Orthodox cross has three bars. The top bar represents the title nailed above Jesus and the short slanting lower bar represents the footrest which points upward to remind believers that Christ points the way to Heaven.

CROSS, SIGN OF (krôs)—The external representation of the Cross of Christ; the mark of Christians since the earliest days of the Christian faith. The Orthodox Church uses the sign of the Cross for all blessings.

CRUETS (krōō'ĕts)—The two bottles on the Oblation Table used for holding the water and wine used in the preparation of the elements for the Holy Eucharist.

CUFFS (kŭfs)—Worn as part of the vestments by deacons and priests. Cuffs remind deacons to put their strength in the right hand of the Lord. Worn by priests, the cuffs are symbolic of the bonds tying the hands of Christ and also symbolize that the priest's hands are tied against sin.

CUPOLA (kū'pŏ là)—The steeple domes found on most Orthodox churches. A church may have a single cupola or as many as thirteen. One dome predominates and signifies Christ as the head of the Church.

D

DALMATIC (dăl măt'ĭk)—The outer vestment worn by deacons during the service.

DEACON (dē'kn)—First of the three orders of Priesthood. Deacons assist priests at Divine Liturgies and other services.

DEAN (dēn)—The elected or appointed supervisor of a district; the senior priest at a Cathedral; the faculty head of a Theological Seminary.

DIKIRI (dī kē'rē)—Double candleholder used by a bishop in blessing worshipers at a Divine Service. It represents the two natures of Christ, human and divine.

DIOCESE (dī'ō sēs)—Territory under the jurisdiction of one bishop.

DISPENSATION (dĭs"pĕn sā'shŭn)—Permission granted by ecclesiastical authority for something not usually permitted by the Canon Law.

DOGMA (dôg'mà)—A truth contained in Scripture or Holy Tradition formulated by the Ecumenical Councils and Fathers of the Church.

DOORS (dōrz)—Most common association is with the three doors of the Iconostas. The north door leads to the Offertory-chapel, the south door to the Sacristy and the center doors are the Royal Doors which have a curtain behind them.

DOXOLOGY (dŏk sŏl'ô jĭ)—A prayer glorifying God.

E

EASTER (ēs'tēr)—Festival commemorating the Resurrection of Christ, known as the Feast of Feasts, greatest church day of the Orthodox year. The Orthodox Easter is celebrated the Sunday following the first full moon of spring. All movable feasts depend upon Easter.

ECTENIA (ĕk'ten ēá)—Also known as Litany; a series of petitions chanted by the priest or deacon with responses by the choir.

ECUMENICAL COUNCIL (ĕk"û mĕn'ĭ kăl koun'sĭl)—An assembly of representatives of the Church legally convoked for the settlement of ecclesiastical affairs, formulating dogmas and making rules of faith and morals. Seven Ecumenical Councils are recognized by the Orthodox Church.

EMINENCE (ĕm'ĭ nĕns)—Title of a Metropolitan.

ENTRANCE (ĕn'trăns)—Solemn procession of the celebrants of Divine Liturgy. The Little Entrance is a procession of the Holy Gospel and the Great Entrance a procession bringing the Holy Gifts from the Oblation Table to the Altar.

EPIGONATION (ê pĭg'û nā shŭn)—An oblong piece of vestment ornament suspended upon the right hip as a symbol of the sword of the spirit. Indicates outstanding service.

EPIPHANY (ē pĭf'à nĭ)—Feast commemorating the manifestation of Christ—the Baptism of Christ and the manifestation of God in the Holy Trinity through the descent of the Holy Spirit. This holy day is also known as Theophany.

EPISCOPATE (ē pĭs'kô pât)—Collectively, the entire body of bishops.

EPISTLE (ê pĭs'l)—A portion of the Scriptures read before the reading of the Gospel at Divine Liturgy.

EUCHARIST, HOLY (ū'kà rĭst)—The Sacrament under which bread and wine become the true Body and Blood of Christ with transubstantiation taking place during the Divine Liturgy.

EVANGELISTS (ê văn'jĕl ĭst)—Inspired writers of the four Gospels—Matthew, Mark, Luke and John.

EVANGELIYE (ē văn je lē'á)—From the Greek, meaning good news; the book of the Gospels used in Divine Services.

F

FAITH (fāth)—The power bestowed by God which enables us to believe what God has revealed.

FASTING (fàst'ing)—Abstaining from certain foods, particularly meat foods.

FASTING DAYS (fàst'ing)—Days and seasons appointed by the Church during which the faithful abstain from meat.

FATHERS of the CHURCH (fä'thĕrs)—Early Christian writers and defenders of the faith.

FEAST (fēst)—A holy day commemorating some saint, some event in the life of Christ or in the life of the Virgin Mary. Easter is the Feast of Feasts and there are twelve other great feasts.

FILIOQUE (fĭl'ĭ o'kwe)—Words inserted in the Nicene Creed by the Roman Church regarding the Holy Spirit.

FRESCOS (frĕs'kōs)—Wall and ceiling murals, painted on the plaster, that adorn the church.

FRUITS of the HOLY SPIRIT (froots—hō'lĭ spĭr'ĭt)—Love, joy, peace, long-suffering, gentleness, goodness, faith, meekness, temperance.

G

GOD (gŏd)—The Supreme, Eternal Almighty Spirit, infinite in all perfections, the creator and governor of all things.

GODFATHER and GODMOTHER (gŏd'-făth'ẽr) (gŏd'mŭth'ẽr)—Sponsors at Holy Baptism; they promise that the godchild is taught the truths of Christian faith.

GOOD FRIDAY (good frī'dā)—The Friday preceding Easter, commemorating Christ's death on the Cross.

GOSPEL (gŏs'pĕl)—Portion of the scriptures read by the priest during Divine Services.

GRACE (grās)—The supernatural gift of God enabling us to attain salvation and obtained mainly by prayer and Sacraments.

GRADUAL (grăd'ū ăl)—Verses from the Psalms or other portions of the Scripture which are sung before the reading of the Epistle.

GUARDIAN ANGELS (gär'dĭ ăn)—Angels divinely appointed at the time of Baptism to guide and protect each individual soul throughout life.

GLORIOUS WEEK (glō'rĭ ŭs wēk)—The week which follows Easter Sunday.

H

HAGIOGRAPHY (hăg''ĭ ŏg'rá fĭ)—Lives of the Saints.

HEAVEN (hĕv'n)—The place and state of perfect blessedness where those who are saved shall be in the full light of God's presence forever.

HELL (hĕl)—The place and state of condemnation where lost souls are tormented eternally.

HERESY (hĕr'ĕ sĭ)—Denial or rejection of a revealed truth by one who has professed Christianity.

HERMIT (hûr'mĭt)—One retiring into a solitary life from religious motives.

HIERARCHY (hī'ẽr är''kĭ)—The higher clergy; the rulers in spiritual matters.

HOLY SPIRIT (hō'lĭ spĭr'ĭt)—Third Person of the Divine Trinity.

HOLY WATER (hō'lĭ wôtẽr)—Water blessed by the priest on the Day of Theophany and on other special occasions. Used to bless persons and things and to drive away evil spirits.

HOLY WEEK (hō'lĭ wēk)—The week preceding Easter, commemorating the sufferings of Christ.

HOPE (hōp)—A supernatural gift of God which enables believers to trust that God will grant eternal life and the means necessary to obtain salvation.

HOSANNA (hô zăn'á)—From the Hebrew, meaning "O Lord, save, we pray."

HOURS (ours)—Simplest form of Orthodox service, performed during the different hours of the day.

I

INCARNATION (ĭn''kär nā'shŭn)—The Christian doctrine that God the Son took to Himself the nature of man.

ICON or IKON (ī'kŏn)—Sacred picture.

ICONOSTAS (ī kŏn'ô stăs)—Image-screen. The high wall covered with sacred pictures that divides the Sanctuary from the Nave of the church.

INCENSE (ĭn sĕns')—Aromatic gum substance burnt in the censer; used during the Divine Services.

INFUSION (ĭn fū'shŭn)—Baptism by pouring water on the head instead of by immersion.

INCLINATION (ĭn klĭ nā'shŭn)—Bowing the head—usually accompanied by crossing—as an unspoken Amen to a prayer.

J

JESUS CHRIST (jē'zŭs krīst)—God the Son, the Second Person of the Holy Trinity. He is one person with two natures, God and man.

JUDGMENT, GENERAL (jŭj'mĕnt jĕn'ẽr ăl)—Judgment of all mankind at the end of the world with the second coming of Christ.

K

KONDAKION (kŏn dȧk'ē ŏn)—Short hymn sung at the Divine Service. There is a different Kondakion for each of the eight tones with special ones for the feast days.

L

LAMB (lăm)—The Host, also known as Agnets. The portion of the bread adhering to the Seal cut from the first prosphora and intended for Consecration.

LANCE (lȧns)—The double-edged, pointed lancet used to cut the Lamb and particles from the prosphora. Also called the Spear.

LENT (lĕnt)—Period of fasting. The Orthodox Church observes four lenten periods during the year with the greatest of these the fasting period before Easter.

LITANY (lĭt′à nĭ)—Petitions recited by the deacon or priest with responses by the choir.

LITURGY, DIVINE (lĭt′ŭr jĭ dĭ vīn′)—Church services celebrating the Holy Eucharist. There are three Liturgies used in Orthodox churches.

LAMPADA (lăm′păd à)—Lamps burning before icons as a mark of honor and as a reminder that the Light of Christ shines through His Saints.

M

MAGNIFICAT (măg nĭf′ĭ kăt)—Hymn sung in honor of the Virgin Mary after the eighth ode of the Canon at Matins.

MANTIA (măn′tē a)—Bishop's mantle, often of purple but may be of some other color, with a long train. Adorned with ribbons, usually red and white, and small bells.

MARTYR (mär′tĕr)—One voluntarily enduring death for the faith.

MASS (màs)—In the Orthodox Church, the Divine Liturgy. In the Western Church it is the service of the Eucharist.

MATRIMONY (măt′rĭ mô nĭ)—Sacrament blessing and sanctifying Christian marriage.

METROPOLITAN (mĕt′rō pŏl′ĭ tan)—Head archbishop of an ecclesiastical province.

MAUNDY THURSDAY (môn′dĭ)—Thursday of Holy Week, marked by the reading of the Twelve Gospels at evening services.

MATINS (măt′ĭns)—Morning Divine Service preceding the Divine Liturgy. Sometimes held on the eve of a church holiday or Sunday.

MITER (mī′tĕr)—Headdress worn by bishops. Archimandrites and some other clergy are also privileged to wear it.

MONASTERY (mŏn′às tĕr ĭ)—Dwelling place of men leading a life of prayer under vows.

MONASTIC VOWS (mô năs′tik vous)—Obedience, poverty and celibacy.

MONK (mŭngk)—One renouncing the world to lead a religious life under monastic vows.

MOTHER OF GOD (muth′ĕr of gŏd)—The Virgin Mary; Jesus, born of her as man, is also truly God.

MYSTERY (mĭs′tĕr ĭ)—A Sacrament, the outward sign of inward grace.

MYRRH (mûr)—Sacred oil used for anointing in the Sacrament of Chrismation.

N

NARTHEX (när′thĕks)—Vestibule area of church leading to the nave.

NATIVITY, FEAST OF (nà tĭv′ĭ tĭ fĕst)—Christmas, commemorating the birth of the Saviour. Observed January 7, New Calendar. Nativity of the Virgin Mary observed September 8; Nativity of John the Baptist observed June 24.

NAVE (nāv)—Center part of the church occupied by worshipers.

NICENE CREED (nī′sēn krēd)—Twelve articles encompassing the Orthodox beliefs.

NUN (nŭn)—Woman who has taken monastic vows.

NUNC DIMITIS (nŭngk dĭ mĭt′ĭs)—Latin words beginning the Song of Simeon sung at Vespers.

N-I-K-A—Initials of the Greek words meaning "By this thou conquer." These initials are stamped on the prosphora.

O

OBLATION (ŏb lā′shŭn)—The preparation of the elements of bread and wine before the beginning of the Divine Liturgy.

OBLATION TABLE (ŏb lā′shŭn tābl)—Table placed against the wall on the left side of the altar where the elements are prepared for the Holy Eucharist before the beginning of the Divine Liturgy.

OFFERTORY (ŏf′ĕr tô rĭ)—Provision, preparation and setting forth on the Altar of the bread, wine and water for Consecration.

ORDINAL (ôr′dĭ năl)—Book containing all the prayers and ceremonies in use at Pontifical services; also the Order of Ordination and Consecration for all grades and dignities of the Church.

ORDINATION (ôr′dĭ nā′shŭn)—Sacrament under which bishops, through the laying on of hands, bestow priesthood on qualified candidates.

ORLETZ (ôr′lĕtz)—The Eagle. A small rug that a bishop stands on during Divine Service. Use is accorded to bishops alone.

OMOFOR (ō′mô fôr)—Bishop's stole which is very broad and which hangs down in front and behind over other vestments. Also called the Pall.

ORAR (ô rär')—The deacon's stole, a long wide band of material worn over the left shoulder, sometimes crossed upon the breast and back.

OKTOICH (ôk'toik)—Service book containing the Canons and hymns of the Eight Tones used during the Short and Great Vespers and Matins.

P

PALL (pôl)—Stole worn by a bishop. Also called Omofor.

PANAGIA (pà nā'gĭ à)—Round or oval image of Christ or the Virgin Mary, richly decorated, worn on the chest by bishops. Means the All-Holy.

PARISH (păr'ĭsh)—Group of faithful united under a properly ordained priest to form a unit of a Diocese and adhering to the tenets of the Church.

PARISH REGISTER (păr'ĭsh rĕj'ĭs tĕr)—Book recording all baptisms, marriages and deaths occurring in a parish.

PASCHAL CANON (păs'kăl kăn'ŭn)—Rule for determining the dates of Easter and other movable feasts.

PASCHAL WEEK (păs'kăl wēk)—The week following Easter.

PASSION WEEK (păsh'ŭn wēk)—Week preceding Easter, commemorating the sufferings and death on the Cross of Christ.

PATEN (păt'ĕn)—Round, flat plate, usually made of silver, upon which the Holy Bread is placed and consecrated.

PATRIARCH (pā'trĭ ärk)—Originally one of the bishops of the four ancient centers of Christianity—Constantinople, Jerusalem, Antioch and Alexandria. Now, the highest dignitary in the church hierarchy.

PECTORAL CROSS (pĕk'tô răl krôs)—Cross worn on the chest of priests and bishops as a mark of their office.

PENANCE (pĕn'ăns)—The Sacrament through which the sins committed after Baptism are forgiven through confession.

PENITENTIAL PSALM (pĕn''ĭ tĕn'shàl säm)—The 50th Psalm of David (the 51st Psalm in English Bibles).

PENTECOST (pĕn'tê kŏst)—Descent of the Holy Spirit upon the Disciples on the fiftieth day after Easter.

PERSECUTIONS (pûr''sê kū'shŭns)—Periods of ill treatment and oppression inflicted because of religious beliefs. In the first three centuries of Christianity there were ten great persecutions.

PONTIFICAL (pŏn tĭf'ĭ kăl)—Relating to the bishops, as Pontifical Services.

PSALTER (sôl'tĕr)—Book of Psalms in the Old Testament used in all Divine Services.

PRESTOL (prĕs'tōl)—The Altar, representing the throne of God in heaven with God himself on it. Also represents the tomb of Christ since His body is placed thereon.

PRIMATE (prī'mât)—Term applied to the ruling archbishop.

PROKIMENON (prô kĭ'mê nŏn)—Verse and refrain which is read and sung before the reading of the Epistle. Also called Gradual.

PROSKOMIDE (prôs ko mī'de)—From the Greek, meaning to bring offering. The first part of the Divine Liturgy consisting of the preparation of bread and wine used in the communion.

PROSPHORA (prôs fôr'à)—Altar Breads used for the Sacrament of Eucharist.

R

READER (rēd'ĕr)—One reading the Psalms, verses and the lesson from the Epistle.

REQUIEM (rē'kwĭ ĕm)—Service for the repose of the souls of the faithful departed.

RESURRECTION OF CHRIST (rĕz''ŭ rĕk'shŭn of krīst)—Christ's rising from the dead.

RITUAL (rĭt'û ăl)—Approved order of a ceremony.

RUBRICS (rōō'brĭks)—From the Latin meaning red. Directions for Divine Services for each Sunday and all holy days, so-called because they are generally printed in red letters.

REVERENCE (rĕv'ĕr ĕns)—A profound bow or a prostration.

S

SABAOTH (săb'â ŏth)—In Hebrew means hosts, hence "The Lord God of Hosts."

SABBATH (săb'àth)—The seventh day of the week, ordered to be kept holy by the Fourth Commandment. The day God rested after creation. The Apostles transferred the obligation to the first day of the week in honor of Christ's resurrection.

SACRAMENT (săk'rà mĕnt)—A mystery—an outward visible sign of an inward invisible grace. The Orthodox Church has Seven Sacraments.

SACRIFICE (săk'rĭ fĭs)—A holy offering. The great Christian Sacrifice is the Holy Eucharist.

SACRISTY (săk'rĭs tĭ)—Room alongside the Sanctuary where the sacred vessels and vestments are kept and where the clergy put on their robes for Divine Services.

SAINT (sānt)—One who has led a pure and holy life and has been inscribed in the list of saints and whose memory is celebrated on a given day.

SAKKOS (săk'kôs)—Proper Eucharistic vestment of bishops.

SANCTUARY (săngk'tŭ ȧ rĭ)—Area of the church, separated from the nave by the iconostas, where the altar stands.

SCHISM (sĭzm)—Separation from the True Apostolic Church. The Great Schism of 1054 divided the Church into East and West.

SEE (sē)—Place where a bishop holds jurisdiction.

SOLEA (sō'lê a)—The raised floor in front of the Iconostas. The middle portion, just in front of the Royal Doors, where Holy Communion is administered, is called the Amvon.

SPOON (spoōn)—Sacred object used to convey the Holy Gifts (body and blood of Christ) into the mouths of communicants.

STOLE (stōl)—Long, narrow vestment worn over the left shoulder by a deacon. A priest's Stole is worn around the neck and joined in front for its entire length, falling low upon the cassock. Neither priests nor deacons can celebrate any service or office without the Stole.

SPONSOR (spŏn'sẽr)—A Godparent at Baptism.

SUNDAY (sŭn'dȧ)—First day of the week, observed by Christians as a day of rest and worship in commemoration of Christ's Resurrection.

T

TABERNACLE (tăb'ẽr nȧ kl)—Receptacle, standing on the Altar, in which the Blessed Sacraments are reserved before conveyance to the sick.

TE DEUM (tē dē'ŭm)—Hymn ascribed to St. Ambrose which is sung at a service of Thanksgiving.

THAUMATURGUS (thô'mȧ tûr gŭs)—Title applied to various saints distinguished for their miracles. A wonder-worker.

THEOLOGY (thê ŏl'ô jĭ)—The science teaching of God and the things of God. Positive Theology explains and interprets the Holy Scriptures and the writings of Church Fathers. Dogmatic Theology proves and defends truths of the faith. Moral Theology explains Christian conduct.

THEOTOKION (thê ŏt'ô kē ŏn)—Hymn in honor of the Mother of God.

THEOTOKOS (thê ŏt'ô kŏs)—The Virgin Mary, Mother of God.

THURIBLE (thū'rĭ bl)—A censer, the vessel in which incense is burned. Also called Kadilo.

TITHES (tĭths)—The tenth part. From earliest times held to be the part due to God.

TONE (tōn)—Standard melody for versicles, troparion and prokimenon, arranged in eight tones, which are sung in continuous cycle throughout the year.

TRADITION, HOLY (trȧ dĭsh'ŭn, hō'lĭ)—The spiritual treasures inherited from the ancestral Holy Fathers, in accord with the scriptures but larger in extent.

TRANSUBSTANTIATION (trăn"sŭb stăn"shĭ ā'shŭn)—In the Holy Eucharist, the changing of bread and wine, at consecration, into the body and blood of Christ.

TREBNIK (trĕb'nĭk)—Book containing the prayers and order of administration of the Sacraments of Baptism, Chrismation and Confession and the Rites of Burial and other services.

TRINITY, HOLY (trĭn'ĭ tĭ, hō'lĭ)—The mystery of faith which teaches that there is One God in Three Divine Persons, the Father, the Son and the Holy Spirit.

TRIKIRI (trĭ'ker ē)—Candleholder for three candles, representing the Holy Trinity, used by the bishop to bestow blessings upon the people.

TRISAGION (trĭs ăg'ĭ ŏn)—The thrice-holy hymn sung at the Divine Liturgy and often said as a prayer: "Holy God, Holy Mighty, Holy Immortal, have mercy on us."

TROPARION (trô pā'rĭ ŏn)—Short hymn sung after the Little Entrance in the Divine Liturgy. There is a different Troparion for each of the eight tones with special ones for each of the feasts.

U

UNCTION (ŭngk'shŭn)—The Sacrament which provides spiritual healing for bodily ills and prepares those critically ill for the better life in Heaven. This Sacrament includes anointment with oil.

UNIATE GREEK CATHOLICS (ū'nē āte)—Those once Orthodox who later acknowledged the authority of the Pope. In church services they follow the Greek rite but adhere to the Roman dogmas.

UNFROCK (ŭn frŏk')—Depriving a priest or bishop of his Orders for a grave offense.

V

VEIL (vāl)—The covering for the Chalice and Paten, used at the beginning and end of the Divine Liturgy.

VERY REVEREND (vĕr'i rĕv'ĕr ĕnd)—Title of address accorded to archpriests.

VESPERS (vĕs'pĕrz)—Even-song. The evening service.

VESSELS, SACRED (vĕs'ĕls, sā'krĕd)—Vessels used in the celebration of the Divine Liturgy.

VESTMENTS (vĕst'mĕnts)—The special garments worn by deacons, priests and bishops in the celebration of Divine Services and in administering the Sacraments.

VIGIL (vĭj'ĭl)—The eve of a holy day.

VOW (vou)—A promise willingly made to God to do something pleasing to Him.

W

WEEKLY CYCLE OF SERVICES (wēk'lĭ sī'kl of sûr'vĭs ĕs)—Each day of the week is consecrated to special memories concerning Christ, the Angels, Apostles, Saints and departed Christians.

WESTERN CHURCH (wĕs'tĕrn chûrch)—The part of the Universal Church which separated in 1054 with the Pope of Rome at the head. Commonly referred to as the Roman Catholic Church.

WINDING SHEET (wīn'dĭng shēt)—A large sheet of velvet with an image of the Entombment of Christ inscribed on it. It is brought out on Good Friday to the center of the church for adoration. On Saturday before midnight it is placed on the Altar and remains there until the Feast of Ascension.

WORSHIP (wûr'shĭp)—Religious services for the glorification of God.

Y

YEAR, ECCLESIASTICAL (yĕr, ĕ klē"zĭ ăs'-tik ăl)—The church calendar which begins the first of September.

Z

ZONE (zōn)—The belt or girdle worn by priests and bishops when robed for celebration of the Divine Liturgy. Made of the same material as the vestments.

Index